When Love Is a Drug

ISBN 9781976935107

I dedicate this book to all in recovery who have gone
before,
all who have walked by my side and
all who are to follow.

Contents

Introduction

When love is a drug it can become an addiction. This book is written to help those who, like me, are addicted to "love". If you suffer from this awful affliction, which can drive you to the point of madness, self-destruction and despair I hope this book will be a point of reference you can return to again and again for sanity, security and peace. Love addiction is obsession, compulsion, distraction and possession; it has nothing whatsoever to do with love. It lives between the realms of total obsession with "other" and total annihilation of "self". It shows itself as fantasy, addiction to the "high", avoidance, and failure to show up for one's own life. There is almost always a fear of true intimacy, coupled with chronic isolation and self-denigration. It encompasses the extremes of acting "out", with total fixation on "other", to acting in with little or no external frame of reference or connection to self or "other". It brings with it broken hearts, warped minds and wasted lives. If unchecked and untreated it can be cross-generational as learned or inherited behaviour. Love addiction is a killer affliction that eats you up from the inside, screws with your gut, your head and your heart. It seems to give you wings but pulls you down further and further from your own core and your own truth.

Preface

I am a recovering love addict and I have written this book in the hope that if you too suffer from this affliction, you can recognise the symptoms and engage with the possible solutions presented in these pages. I know only too well the pain that accompanies love addiction and the resultant chaos and devastation that follows in its wake. Only those that suffer from the same dis-ease can fully understand the impact it has on our lives, as it affects us in mind, body and soul. Our families and friends, if we have any, look on from the safe shore of "normality" at what can only seem like a mess, a wasted life, simply being unlucky in love, or terminally unfortunate in affairs of the heart. They fail to grasp, as do we, the enormity of the problems we grapple with daily; our inability to truly love ourselves, our lack of deep and meaningful long-term relationships, whether with family, friends, work colleagues or partners and the depth of loneliness and feelings of isolation that we are plagued by. We are often the black sheep of the family who do not fit in anywhere; we may as well be from Mars as we fail to truly connect with anyone else on the planet. Despite all of this, I believe we can recover from love addiction if we first recognise the symptoms, then seek help from either a 12-step treatment centre, recovery group (such as Relationships Anonymous (RA) or Sex and Love Addicts Anonymous (SLAA), Co-dependents Anonymous (CoDA) a therapist trained in Love Addiction or have some sort of spiritual awakening and get honest with how we really feel. I personally could not have done this journey on my own; I needed the identification from other love addicts and a set of simple tools of recovery to use to get well. I also needed to learn the language to describe my life and lack of connection. This book has been written in the hope that you too can get identification and make the journey into recovery yourself so that you finally have a life worth living. I hope you find this book useful as a guidepost, pointing the way out from your isolation and desperation into the sunlight of the spirit. You need to know you are not alone, there are thousands of us around the world who have recognised this affliction and have sought help, improving the quality of our lives and our relationships exponentially as a direct result of engaging in the process of recovery.

The book begins with my own personal journey through my relationships and how my attitude to "love" changed when I recognised my own love addiction. This is then followed by more stories from other love addicts.

The book continues with useful information about how to recognise and deal with withdrawal symptoms, which can occur when you leave an addictive and/or abusive relationship. I then look at the disease within the disease – social, emotional and sexual anorexia {Anorexia in love addiction has nothing to do with the avoidance of food, but instead with the avoidance of life, love and relationship whether to self or to others} that is often at the core of love addiction. At its simplest it is the disease of "not doing" and "not engaging" also termed "love avoidance". I attempt to explain how it shows itself and how to grow emotionally and spiritually so that you no longer have to live in an anorectic way but can begin to fully engage with yourself, your life and with others. I personally have not found this journey easy and in times of extreme stress or pain I can return to my default position of isolation, which is my safety blanket that protects me from the world of pain that I inhabited for so much of my life. However difficult the journey has been, it has been so worthwhile. Now, instead of living in pain and isolation permanently, I may visit it occasionally and when the feeling of being overwhelmed passes, I soon return to connection with my source, myself and with others. I encourage you to get help; you are worth it, it can and does get better. You can, little by little, melt the walls of the castle of ice that you have built up around you and bask in the warmth of the sun. We need to learn how to be our own best friend, lover, confidant and counsellor, we need to listen to our own truth and begin to act upon it. We begin by learning to love and value ourselves and to believe in our own dreams, hopes and wishes. We learn to esteem ourselves and to practice self-care on a moment-by-moment basis. My hope in writing this book is that you start on your journey to self-love, self-respect and freedom from active love addiction and sexual, social and emotional anorexia. We do not realise that the only person who can help us is **us**. In Love, hope and fellowship.

Chapter 1

My Story - The Damage

Many love addicts, but by no means all, experienced some form of sexual or emotional abuse or abandonment in childhood. Often one or more of the parents of the love addict were themselves love addicted, or addicted to mood altering substances, gambling or work, or suffered from some form of mental and/ or emotional difficulty. Growing up in such a household the child's reality is often denied, and subsequently suffers emotional harm because of this. This harm is then often experienced as fear, shame and confusion. The message that accompanies these feelings is that the child cannot trust its own version of reality. Without a solid core the child fails to mature emotionally, and the roots of love addiction are born. Low self-esteem, self-love and self-care proliferate alongside the excessive use of fantasy, focus on "other" and subsequent disconnect from self. I grew up in such an environment in a male dominated working class family in the north of England in the 1960's. I remember the feeling of being alive, present and happy until the age of four. I felt free, innocent and unencumbered with life's woes. I walked in the light and

I remember it was beautiful. I was joyful, and it felt good to be me. I was free of limitation, the voices of judgment and shame, unafraid of shining my light. Maybe a child psychologist would say that a child of four would not be capable of feeling these emotions. I was certainly unable to name or give voice to them, it is my adult self that does so. However, this fact makes them no less real. All I can truly say is I spent my days smiling, talking, laughing, meeting the world head on, free of all negativity and judgment. Free from fear, shame and worry and most of all free to just be me. I have been told I was a little ray of sunshine and spent my days saying "hello" to everyone who passed by.

We were poor, but we did not know it. My parents both worked, Dad had 2 jobs, Mum had one plus she did most of the parenting and all the cooking and cleaning. We lived in a two-bedroom maisonette with no garden, very little space and even less money. When I was 3 Dad got a job in a car factory, so we moved out into the relative countryside about 30 miles outside of the city centre. We were given a 3-bed council house with a garden. Both parents still worked. Life was easier. All my siblings went to school, so I spent a lot of time on my own, as I didn't start school until I was nearly 6. My Mum was a complicated character. She was very warm and loving, generous of heart and encouraging of my efforts to learn. She was herself a frustrated academic who was the oldest daughter in a family of 10 surviving children and had to leave school at age 14 to help provide for her younger siblings. She was bright, and most days was able to complete the times crossword. However, she also had a darker side. She had massive mood swings, was always on some tablet or other from the doctors, suffered hugely from depression and at one point had to be hospitalized for it. I believe she was an undiagnosed bipolar with alcoholic tendencies. She most certainly had a change of character half way down the first glass of wine. My father felt quite remote to me. I never really felt particularly emotionally connected to him, although I did argue a lot with him regarding his views about race and society. He held diametrically opposing views to me. His favourite saying to me was "modulate" as I was too loud, too much, too everything for his quiet disposition. I took after my Mum who was much more fiery and volatile than my father who was retiring and emotionally aloof. They often argued, especially if alcohol was involved and that is when his rage could erupt if he had drunk too much whiskey.

When I was 4 something occurred that totally changed the direction of my life. I was sexually abused and awakened by someone not much older than me, someone who knew no better, someone who was himself lost in the pain of being sensitive to life. Some would say that it was just two children exploring their bodies, but for me it had a massive impact on the rest of my life. I was taken from the sunlight of the spirit into the shadows, from ease to dis-ease; it fractured my psyche and took away my innocence. It altered forever how I related to myself and to the world. It brought with it shame, secrets and hiding, the feeling of it not being ok to be me. I felt defective, dirty, broken and I spent the next 50 years trying to return to that place of innocence. It shaped my whole being. My abuser awoke in me my sexuality way before I was ready, willing or able to deal with it or the fallout that came as a consequence of it being prematurely ignited. I do not blame him, he was looking for love and attention, and he meant me no harm. It did, however, have a profound effect on my life. I learned that my body was not my own, that I did not have a voice and that my body had currency and power over the opposite sex. It set up some incredibly powerful beliefs that have persisted throughout most of my life. I believed that I had no choice, no voice, that I was invisible, that my needs were not important; I learned that the way for me to survive was by disappearing, splitting off, and abandoning myself as I felt abandoned. It wasn't so much about what happened to me, the details are almost irrelevant. What is important are the patterns and beliefs that were formed then. Patterns and beliefs that subconsciously ran my life from that point on. Every decision I made, every thought I had emanated from a place of dis-ease. My fear was ever present. It was not just a knot in my stomach and a retraction of my spirit, it was an interruption to the flow, a dis-connect from my own truth and myself. From the age of four I ceased being present in my own life, I became instead a spectator, once removed, watching a movie of my life rather than present within it. I felt abandoned so abandoned myself. I felt pain so caused myself more pain. It was not Ok to be me. I developed coping strategies to deal with the trauma and resultant feelings of shame and brokenness. These strategies that helped me to survive, such as acting as if, disappearing, fantasy, splitting off from my own body, invisibility, bullying and burying feelings, became the prison within which I lived. I was over sensitive, highly tuned to the emotions of others and progressively more disconnected from my own. I became a chameleon, disappearing into whatever I thought you wanted me to be. I adopted the belief that I was defective, bad, less than. My innocence was lost and in its place festered fear, shame, self-hatred and self-doubt. I became disconnected from grace. I was driven by a host of unconscious drives and urges; the need to forget, the need to stay out of reality, the need to disappear. It set up a pattern of living in fantasy, often involving sexual content or romance. I lost myself in books, daydreaming and films and took my head and body somewhere else. By the time I got to school I started acting out rather than acting in. I continued this behavior with cousins and other boys in the neighbourhood. I felt noticed, important and wanted, but for all the wrong reasons. My feelings of shame and self-loathing increased due to my acting out and took me further and further from a feeling of wholeness, deeper into the darkness. I have mourned for that little girl all my life.

Most of the adults I have spoken to who suffered trauma in their early childhood can identify with most of these feelings. What differs is how individuals deal with the feelings. Some act out, and become very promiscuous, some act in and deny themselves a full life and some oscillate between the two and do both. I woke up today and I was back in the place of needing to hide. I continue to work hard to change the beliefs that I held for most of my life "it's not ok to be me" "it's not ok to shine, if you shine they will talk about you, judge you,"

"you are dirty and defective", "you are defined by your past not your present." I have worked tirelessly to replace the negative self-talk with other more positive thoughts such as "you were only a child", "you were not responsible", "it is great to be me", "if I shine I allow others to shine", "I am a good, decent person and all is well".

I was a bright, studious, academic and sporty child and yet I felt ashamed every single day of my school life. I was worried and fearful in case someone from my early school life noticed me or made a derogatory comment about me. From the age of 8 I fought boys rather than kissed them. I had no boyfriends as a teenager up until the age of 17 yet my past still haunted me, as did my reputation. What I needed to do was face the boys down, give them some stick back and shut them up. What I did instead was stay quiet, internalize, continue to have no voice and stay in shame. My internal battle, the need to succeed and shine fought with the need to stay hidden and to disappear into the background. My hiding took the form of eating too much and gaining weight as a teenager, which of course only increased my feelings of shame and low self-esteem. When I was 16 I met my sister in law for the first time and she told me she had never met anyone as "good" as me before. I didn't smoke, drink, go out with boys, swear or do any of the usual teenage stuff. I was studious and serious about life. For my 16th birthday I was bought a pen and had to babysit for my younger sister who was born when I was 12. I did not complain. I passed my 8 O levels with flying colours. I enjoyed learning, was part of the top set at school and a member of the hockey, netball, swimming and athletics team. I remember feeling self-conscious and yet I suspect if you asked others what I was like they would no doubt have said I was confidant and a good all-rounder. The internal and external did not match. I was good at acting as if. The shame and feelings of being dirty and not good enough were still there and I was reminded about my past every day I attended school, every time I was in a class with any of the boys I acted out with, or any time I raised my hand to ask a question. Friends around me started sleeping with boyfriends from the age of 16, I felt sick at the mere thought of it. I was shy and very self-conscious.

At 17, half way through my A levels, something changed within me. I went to my first proper party and someone spiked my drink. It was the first time I had drunk anything more than a shandy. I remember going to the party and the next thing I can recollect is waking up in bed the next day with my Mother shouting at me, as I had been sick all over the covers. I had gone instantly into "blackout" (where chunks of time disappear from memory after imbibing alcohol), I do not know what happened at the party or how or when I got home. It was a sign of things to come but instead of putting me off I died my hair auburn, got a perm and started working in a nightclub in Liverpool. I met my first boyfriend there who was an alcoholic depressive. We did not have sex as I was far too frightened to do that, but it did set up a pattern of me choosing emotionally unavailable and damaged individuals. Most of my partners from that point on were addicts or alcoholics who had childhood trauma of their own and who needed saving. That first boyfriend was 6 years older than me and I was flattered and grateful that he noticed me. He was totally unsuitable for me but as I had no criteria due to my own lack of self-worth and low self-esteem, it never occurred to me to say no to his advances. I joined him in his drinking and continued to have "blackouts". Thankfully the relationship did not last long as he was not OK with me saying no to sex.

At 18 I met the first love of my life, Tommy, who was a gentle, loving man. A month or so after we met we both went off to Europe. He went with a friend of his backpacking on the train and I went for 3 months to St

Tropez on a working holiday. I went with a friend of mine called Paula and two of her sisters and her sister's boyfriend. We made and sold sandwiches on the beach every day, had far too much to drink every night (the blackouts continued) and went home with more money than we left with. Tommy had made a passing comment that he might travel down to St Tropez on his way around Europe and I was on high alert and tenterhooks every day for the first month in case he made it. It was my first experience of that delicious yet agonizing yearning for other, alongside the growing hole that their absence created. It was my first brush with love addiction. I really hadn't known him very long, but the need to completely merge with him and lose myself in him was utterly overwhelming. I had just finished my A levels and found out that I had passed all 3, albeit with lower grades than expected. I was offered a place to read history at a good northern university, but when Tommy asked me not to go I agreed without a second thought. I had no idea how much I was limiting my life by making that decision, I threw away the opportunity without even a second thought. No one in my family of origin had at that point ever been to university, so it was a big thing for me to just throw it away, yet because he asked me, I did it. I abandoned myself, my life and my hopes and dreams for a relationship. Instead I started training to be an accountant at a local college but hated it and left to work for the local council as a temp and then in a permanent admin role. I was bored in the role but being with Tommy was more important than my own personal happiness. We were together 3 years. I tried very hard to conform to "normal" life. We rented a flat together, we both worked, we went for meals, did martial arts together and drank at weekends. When I met some " alternative " people, who had wild parties, took drugs and sang and played music, my spirit soared, but I could not take Tommy with me, so the relationship ended. I went off to Greece for 3 months and when I came back went to university in Manchester. I was now 21. I did not know it at the time, but this was the last relationship I was to have with someone who was not an addict for over 30 years.

Chapter 2

Lost in Excess

Once at university I lost myself in everything that was going on around me. I drank too much, tried every drug under the sun and listened to great music. It was the first time in my life I had ever lived on my own. I was 21 but felt like I was17. I hung out with the arts students even though I was doing a BSC in Management Science, which included economics, accountancy, mathematics, history, sociology and psychology. I loved the sociology and psychology and hated the rest. I started going out with a guy called Nathan, who was 3 years younger than me. He was a gentle, intelligent person but the main thing we had in common was that we both liked experimenting with drugs. He had experienced a difficult childhood and was brought up by his Grandmother; he was never violent or abusive to me. This was the first relationship I had been in where I felt I had the power and control due to the age difference and difference in life experience. I liked having the illusion of control. I was not physically attracted to Nat, he was smaller than me, wore glasses and probably weighed less than me, but what I did like was being in charge, having the illusion of control and power within the relationship. The mixture of drink, drugs and the control made me forget most of my childhood trauma. I cannot say I was happy, but I wasn't locked in pain or self-consciousness as I had been growing up. It was a neutral, numb sort of space, I guess in a way I felt safe as I did not feel threatened by him physically or emotionally.

At the end of our first year we both dropped out of university and ended up squatting in Bristol in a three-story house. The lower floor was where the criminals lived, punks lived on the middle floor and on the top floor were the hippies. I lived on the top floor but also hung out with the "crims". Whilst there I learned about free festivals such as Stonehenge and as I made wine someone suggested I make a load and take it down there. When I landed at my first festival, Stonehenge, within half an hour I had a beer in one hand, a spliff in the other and copious amounts of opium in my system. I couldn't believe my eyes. There were people queuing for lines of coke, people wandering around naked or semi naked, it felt like I'd been transported back to what I imagined Woodstock was like in the 60's. I did not realize at the time that my hedonism was simply a coping strategy, a way to deaden the memory of what happened to me in childhood, to shut off the pain. It wasn't about having a good time or partying, although it seemed it at the time, it was a way to deal with the pain of being me. I lost myself to excess, which although stopped me from thinking for a while, brought with it a pain of its own. Because of my lifestyle choices I began to feel the old familiar feeling of shame and degradation again, which I experienced as a constant knot in my stomach and growing dis-ease within myself. Once again, I had abandoned myself for a male, as my love addiction denied me the ability to question any of my decisions or those of my partner. At the start of the year I was sitting in a room with hundreds of other students being told "you are the future of this country" and by the end of it I was sat in a field bombed out of my head going nowhere fast. The relationship didn't last, and I was soon onto the next one.

After experiencing my first free festival I went to live on the road with a band of travelling people. They adopted me as their official wine maker. I met a traveller called Barry who was on the run for going AWOL from the army 10 years earlier. Barry took even more drugs than me but mostly marijuana and drink with the occasional party drug. He was a sex addict and had several more women on the go at the same time as me, which I found out after I left him. I turned my life upside down for him but was not addicted to him, just excited by the freedom that living on the road offered me and in love with my "alternative" lifestyle. After I left him I saw a couple more guys then settled into a relationship with someone much more dangerous to me. His name was BOB, a former biker, who injected heroin and speed, had violent outbursts, was incredibly controlling and drank huge amounts of alcohol. He was very charismatic. My love addiction really took hold of me when I was with Bob and my sex addiction was triggered for the first time. Up until this point sex had been OK but was not a huge factor in my relationships because of my fear of emotional and sexual intimacy. With Bob sex was a drug in itself. The wild sex sessions, fuelled by drugs and alcohol, were incredibly addictive, they took me to a whole new level, but the comedowns were horrendous. There were physical symptoms, but these were nowhere near as bad as the emotional pit of shame I sank into afterwards. I was with him on and off for about 2 years, it took me three attempts to leave him and it was incredibly difficult to do so. The last time I left him I hitched to a town in the shires and went to live up on a gypsy site just out of town with some other hippies I had met previously. My love addiction was progressing and each situation I was in and each partner I was with harmed my self -esteem and threatened my safety even more than the last. This is the nature of love addiction, it always gets worse, never better. Unchecked it can cause pain, destruction and even death. I am extremely grateful that I survived this period of my life; some love addicts are not so lucky.

Once I managed to get away from Bob life was much calmer for a while. I was in my black period, where I hid from the world. I had long dark hair, which covered most of my face; all my clothes were long, dark and baggy, I was hiding from the world and from men. Even in this place and space I found men who were attracted to me. I wanted them to leave me alone; I really did look horrendous and could not understand how anyone could be attracted to me in that state. Whilst living up the gypsy site, firstly in a VW camper on bricks with no wheels and then in a homemade "bender" made of willow poles and tarpaulin, and a milk carton with a plate welded on its side for a stove, I met my next partner, Tommy. Tommy had been a devotee of an American Guru, had a great sense of style and was well liked by many. He was an untreated manic-depressive, which I did not find out until after I had moved into town with him. Tommy was a gentle soul, but his manic depression was horrendous to live with. When he was "up" he took copious amounts of drugs and hardly slept or ate, he had great ideas and knew lots of people to party with. At some point he would flip into mania and become very paranoid and confused. All of this was preferable to the depressed Tommy who could not speak, stayed in bed all day, put on weight and seemed to have the weight of the world on his shoulders. At no point did I think about myself, what I needed or wanted, I still had no criteria about what to look for in a partner other than he was there and he wanted me. My self-esteem, self-care and self-love was still almost non-existent. At one point I even took all his drugs so that he couldn't. I wanted him to see how badly the drugs affected me so that he would stop and consider what he was doing to himself, but of course it didn't work and was exactly what a love addict would do.

We eventually got a council flat and I started training as a vegetarian chef once a month in Manchester. This gave me a short respite from the drugs and the madness back at home. I was with "normal" people who had homes, husbands, children and it reminded me who I really was and how far I had slipped away from my real self. Tommy went off to work at Glastonbury festival as a litter picker and met a woman from New Zealand whilst there. They both came back to the Shire and lived in the garage of our flat. They would come in and use all my food up every time I went away, do yoga every morning in front of the garage and come in and use the facilities when they needed to. I felt like I could not say no as the flat was in Tommy's name. I had no voice. It literally felt like I had lunacy all around me. After a few months she left him and continued on her travels. He then pleaded with me to take him back, but I was unable to do so. A very small sliver of self-respect had begun to grow within me due to the vegetarian training and the time spent around "normal" people. Tommy wrote me page after page of apologies and pleadings, which he had done on numerous occasions before, but this time I didn't cave in to his demands. I knew I could not go back into the madness again with him, I even moved out of the flat for a while and stayed on his brother's sofa but did go back eventually. He would threaten to take his own life regularly if I did not take him back, as he had done many times before. I carried on my training and whilst I was up in Manchester, just before Tommy's 30th birthday, he committed suicide. He had told me in one of his down times that he had made a promise to himself when he was a child, that if he still felt the way he did as a child by the time he reached 30, he would kill himself. I just happened to be the one who was with him when he got there. I fell into a deep well of depression. I felt guilty, ashamed, judged by people who didn't know the whole story and I also judged myself. I lost myself in drink and marijuana. The "party" drugs no longer appealed to me, I wanted substances to deaden my pain, not stimulate my brain. The Shire was awash with heroin back then, I had tried smoking it once at university but absolutely hated the effect it had on me, so did not go down that route, thank God, as I have no doubt whatsoever that if I had taken heroin during this period of my life, I would not be alive today. My main drug of choice was marijuana topped up with booze. The council let me stay in the flat and as I had nowhere else to go, that is what I did. My parents later told me that they really feared for my life and sanity at this time as they knew Tommy was a deeply disturbed soul and they prayed he did not take me with him. Thankfully, suicide has never been an option for me. However, there were times throughout this period when I truly did not know how I was going to survive the constant pain and depression that I was suffering. My love addiction had taken me to a new all-time low.

Chapter 3

Dawn of the Ice Maiden

I was now 26. The next few years were lost in a haze of booze and smoke. I was just about functioning but not fully alive. Every day felt like it was a struggle to get through. I had to deaden my emotions as much as I possibly could, as it all felt too raw. Someone described it as having too few layers of skin and the volume of life turned up to the maximum. I was lonely, isolated inside my own head and depressed. I had zero self-esteem or self-love, and every single day felt like I was wading through thick black treacle. I self-medicated with alcohol and marijuana. I know most people would have gone to the doctors to get anti-depressants, but I have always been averse to taking tablets of any kind because of seeing what my mother went through. Luckily, I had lovely neighbours next-door, Paula and Paul, who often invited me in for food or a game of scrabble, but other than that I did very little socializing. My pilot light was turned down very low; my days were about existing, not living, and I dragged myself through each day as best I could. I look back on the person I was in this period of my life. I was completely emotionally and sexually shut down, I was functioning in terms of work or career at about a hundredth of my capacity, I was always either stoned or topped up with booze to deaden the pain of being me and where all my decisions had taken me. I felt like I had a mountain to climb without the will or the energy to do so. I knew I needed to connect back in with life but it all seemed so difficult and so far away. I felt like I was locked behind a glass tower, no one was able to get in and although I could see life going on around me, I was totally incapable of fully engaging with it. I felt like a shell, going through the motions. I even referred to myself as the "ice maiden".

After going through the motions for about 18 months I knew I had to get on with my life again, so I went back and finished my vegetarian training and started teaching night classes in vegetarian cookery at the local college. I half-heartedly ran my own vegetarian business, but I was too stoned most of the time to make a success of it. Music came back into my life at this time. I was at a party one night, singing along with the tunes, and someone suggested I should be in a band. They knew someone who knew someone and before I knew it I had joined a band with a fantastic woman called Sheena and a lovely guy called Bob. We called the band "All aboard the 4" and wrote all our own songs, some of which were quite good. They both played acoustic guitar and I sang and played percussion. Writing lyrics really helped me to start to get back in touch with my buried emotions. In terms of relationships, it was the only time in my life I slept with a married man and felt dreadful about it and stopped. It was purely about wanting to be held, nothing more, and not knowing how to get that without sex. I wasn't in any recovery program back then and did not know how to nurture myself. I was not ready for a real relationship, so chose someone who was emotionally and physically unavailable. It was excruciatingly painful each time he left, and I always felt worse, so I stopped it after a few months and went back to emotional and sexual isolation.

The next man I got involved with I met on a train on my way back from Manchester. I smoked back then and followed him out into the hallway of the train. He offered me a light, we began talking and before he left the train gave me his number. It turned out that he was a doctor, lived near Heathrow and was he was very attractive. I had a brief affair with him but stopped after he told me he was engaged! Just as it was when I was at school, there was a huge emotional disconnect from myself and my life and the outside world. I was still "going through the motions" externally, on autopilot, seeming to connect to people through music and my vegetarian cooking, but all the while living in an internal hell, where no one truly got in. I could vaguely see people but could not touch or be touched emotionally. The closest I came to allowing anyone in was to be physically close to a male, which would temporarily satisfy my need to be physically held. It did not, however, challenge my emotional isolation. It was a very cold, desperately lonely, place to live. There was no real joy, only drug induced numbness, which was the best I could hope for at this time. Marijuana deadened my pain and senses, and I was grateful for it. The price for the numbness was very high. I had chosen drugs rather than continue with the band. I love reading and learning but was not able to focus for very long, my brain just felt like "mush". My vegetarian catering business failed, as I didn't have the focus or the energy to take it anywhere. I was teaching vegetarian cookery at the local college and could have gone on to write my own recipe books, but just didn't have the energy. So yes, I survived, and functioned up to a point, but everything was a slog and any time I spent "straight" was very difficult.

I then met the father of my children, Robert, who was painting the stairwell of the council flat where I lived. My first impression of him was that he was angry, uncouth, rude and nasty. I walked past him and banged in to him slightly with my bag. I apologized and all I got in return was a glare and a growl. A few days later he knocked on my door to ask me what colour I wanted my door painted. I said, "anything but red" and a stunted conversation began about why not red (I grew up supporting Everton whose colour is blue, whilst their rival, Liverpool's colour is red). Within a few months he had moved in to my flat. Back then I literally had no criteria for choosing a man to have a relationship with other than the fact that he was physically there and wanted me. I look back on this version of me and see a woman with very low self-esteem, little or no self-awareness or ability to value herself in any way. I was still in emotional pain from what happened to Tommy, self-medicated with booze and marijuana, depressed, and in denial about my unresolved childhood issues. I was a broken woman who attracted a broken man. Robert had suffered physical and mental abuse at the hands of his mentally ill surrogate Mum. He had a lot of unresolved emotional pain and resultant anger issues.

I was extremely hormonal when we met and to my utmost surprise my body was screaming out for a child. Within a couple of years my first child was on the way and 2 years later my second. Although I most certainly did not feel emotionally ready for a child, I was 29 but felt like a 17-year-old, my body was ready for one and it dragged the rest of me kicking and screaming towards motherhood. I have never been a "baby" sort of woman. When my younger sister was born I was 12 and I was holding her one time when she started to cry. One of my uncles said, "you must have pinched her" jokingly, but me being an extremely shy, oversensitive soul, took it to heart and literally never went near her or any other baby again until I had my own. I was a reluctant mother, but once my beautiful baby girl was here on the planet, everything inside me changed. I knew my days of smoking marijuana were numbered. I would love to say that the minute I knew I was pregnant I stopped, but I didn't. I tried with every ounce of my own willpower to stop smoking weed every single day of my pregnancy. I would last until around 3pm then my body and mind would scream out for it. Anyone who thinks that smoking pot is not addictive has obviously not smoked it every day for years and then tried to stop. I didn't drink through the pregnancy other than the odd Guinness, which continued after she was born, but the thought of being 24/7 without any painkillers inside of me was terrifying.

Chapter 4

Begin to Surrender

When my daughter Sophia was one a local lady called Hetty started a group called Relationships Anonymous (RA) based on a book she had read and invited me along. I think there were about 6 of us at the inaugural meeting at the local well woman centre. The book talked about 10 steps to turn your life around concerning relationships. At the second meeting Hetty said it was going to be a 12-step meeting instead, run along the lines of Alcoholics Anonymous (a group of individuals who meet to deal with their alcohol addiction which began in the 1930's in America and is now worldwide with millions of members). I was really angry about this change in focus and balked hugely as it talked about needing a spiritual solution to deal with the disease of love addiction. I did not like the thought of being labeled an "addict" (even though I had been addicted to marijuana for years). Despite my protestations I continued to attend the meeting, as something inside of me knew that I needed to grab this opportunity as a drowning person grabs a life raft. After the first couple of weeks I was able to tell Robert where I was going. I had originally told him I was going to see a friend, but something about the strength within the group, that I was no longer alone with my struggles, enabled me to become stronger and less afraid of him and more able to speak my truth. Within a month I was leaving the literature around for him to read and within 6 weeks of attending my first meeting I had completely stopped smoking marijuana and tobacco, which was incredibly brilliant. I knew I would never make it out of the relationship if I continued to smoke. Every time I tried to stop I would get so far and then fall back into the "I'll do it tomorrow" syndrome.

I could feel my self-esteem growing along with my self-awareness. I still had very little or no self-love, but my level of self-care was increasing, it was at last in its infancy. At least I remembered I had a "self" that I needed to care for. Paradoxically, I was more than willing and able to care for my daughter, which makes sense, as I had been "other" referenced throughout my childhood due to my focus on my mother. I was always able to tell you how she was; I was hyper-vigilant about her moods but disconnected from my own feelings. In my mid 20's I had read the book "women who love too much" and could not relate to it at all. I was obviously in complete denial about my relationship issues and love addiction. When I read it again after attending RA, I could see myself on every page. My denial was shattered, my memories around my childhood abuse came flooding back and although it was painful, like a comfort blanket had been ripped from me, part of me felt totally relieved that my "blindness" to my afflictions had gone and the light of truth was starting to shine in my darkest places. I recognized that my need to attach was matched only by my inability to form true lasting relationships. This need kept me in, and returning to, emotionally, physically, mentally and spiritually damaging relationships. I began to understand all of this over the next couple of years, but it was not until 12 years later that I truly began to comprehend the true depth of my love addiction.

I continued to attend the meetings and remained in the relationship with Robert for a further 2 ½ years in which time I also had a son called Jack. My external life started to improve slowly. I got involved with the local musician's union and became secretary for a year, earning a small stipend, but more importantly it helped my self-esteem to grow outside of my relationship. I also got involved with a women's musical organization out of which came a women's choir run by a brilliant woman from Devon. I also started a band with another lady who remains a friend today. The driving force behind the Musicians Union and the women's organization was a lady called Roberta, who I ran into one day in the town when I was very down. She took me for coffee and realized how low I was in my relationship and it was her belief and encouragement that got me out of my door and involved in these ventures. I believe I was also suffering from undiagnosed Post Natal Depression. Being involved with these organisations helped me enormously to start to remember who I was, an intelligent, capable woman who has much to give and share with others. When the choir stopped I decided to go and get some voice training with an inspirational lady who taught freeing the voice techniques. I learned about how to work with the voice and how to sing from the heart. I also learned lots of songs to sing with choirs and games and exercises to help people "find their voice". I started running singing for non-singer's classes at the local college and out of this started a women's choir and then with Roberta a community choir. I was the musical director and she the secretary and treasurer. We did that together for 3 years and I continued for two more after she left. By the end there were over 60 regular members. We did concerts and performances all over the region and there was a great sense of fun and community. My connection to "other" seemed on the outside to be better and I could at long last look people in the eyes because I was no longer a drug addict, but my alcohol consumption had started to increase.

My family and I were now living in a 3-bed council house in a nice part of town with a lovely garden. My relationship with Robert was still very unhealthy and draining and had deteriorated still further after the birth of our son. When the children were 31/2 and 1 ½ my partner, the children's father, became violent towards me and I told him to leave. My self-esteem was still shaky but growing so I was able to say it and mean it. I would no longer tolerate any such behavior towards my children or myself. I would like to say that the following years were filled with happiness and bliss, but, the next 2-½ years were financially and emotionally the hardest of my life up to that point. I was depressed and started to drink more to cope. I could no longer bury my emotions under a haze of smoke, so my nerves jangled horrifically. They were too close to the surface and when thoughts of my difficult childhood came flooding in I had only one place left to turn – alcohol. I would never drink before 7pm and could not afford to drink as much as I wanted to, but booze started to take hold of me mentally. I used it as a crutch to cope with my situation. I hated watching soaps on TV, yet I started to watch them avidly during this period. I used them, along with the alcohol to escape my reality. My best friends were "electric valium" and red wine. It was during this period that I started to experience blackouts again as I had when I was 17. It was quite funny at first as I could laugh it off when I couldn't remember phoning someone the night before and they would ring me and start talking about something I had no recollection of; but when I couldn't remember where I had parked my car the night before, it became slightly less funny. The consequences of the blackouts got a lot more serious for me when I slept with someone and had absolutely no recollection of doing so whatsoever until they asked me why I was distant with them.

From that point on I was increasingly more terrified to drink and became suspicious and paranoid, not wanting to engage with anyone. I knew I needed help but didn't know what was wrong with me. I poured the last of my beer down the sink and gave away all my wine (I knew I could not drink it but could not bear to pour it away!). I was terrified to drink but knew instinctively that the fear of taking another drink would fade and that I would drink again. I also knew I could not do healthy or intimate relationships so went to see a counsellor at a treatment centre in the Shire that deals with alcohol and drug addiction. My counsellor told me that I was an alcoholic. He said there was no difference between the people in the centre that were being treated for drug and alcohol addiction, and me. When he said those words to me it felt like the gates of doom had closed around me. Since stopping class B drugs 5 years previous and class A drugs 5 years before that, alcohol had been my only crutch. It had seemed like a comforting friend who wrapped its arms around me when life got tough. I always looked forward to the de-stress that happened after that first sip where my shoulders would relax, and I would feel like I could breathe again. Part of me knew the counsellor was right, it made sense, but another part of me railed against the idea. The thoughts that went through my head were "shit, how can I live without alcohol?" "I will never be able to enjoy myself again, my life is over". "Life will be so boring and depressing". "How will I get through the day or sleep?" The counsellor countered all these fears with "look at your life now it is in chaos, you are in pain, how successfully are you living your life now?" "Do you enjoy being in blackout?" "You will be able to live the life you deserve and build a future for you and your children". "After the first week you will sleep better than you have done in years". After weeks of arguing back and forth I relented and went to my first

Alcoholics Anonymous meeting.

The Counsellor had arranged for me to meet a lady called Macy in the train station in another part of the Shire as I refused to go to a local meeting in case someone recognized me. I turned up 20 minutes late as my life was completely unmanageable back then and we went into a meeting in the crypt of a church (which I hated), everyone smoked (which I hated – ex smokers are always the most vehemently anti-smoking!) and when they stopped the meeting to say "welcome to the newcomer who is at her first meeting" I wanted the ground to open up and swallow me and vowed I would never set foot inside another meeting as long as I lived. When I went to my next counseling session I recanted my sorry tale and the counsellor had the gall to laugh! He kept on at me to try again, as every meeting is different, and after a few weeks I relented. This time I went to my local meeting. At this meeting no one at all spoke to me or acknowledged me in any way so at the next counseling session I told the counsellor in no uncertain terms where he could stick the meetings as I would never ever go to another one again. I was still not drinking at this time, mostly out of fear, but the thought of taking another drink had started to creep back in to my mind. I had also started to minimize the horror of where my last drink had taken me, as it had done many times before. The shiny coloured liquid was starting to reach out to me in my dreams or when walking around the supermarket and I knew it was more a matter of when rather than if I would take another drink. About a week later the strangest thing happened. I was stone cold sober and had not imbibed any other mood-altering substances whatsoever, and yet I found myself sat at an Alcoholics Anonymous meeting on a Wednesday evening, almost "coming to" as if coming out of a blackout. I still have no recollection of how I got there, or of arranging a baby sitter but there I was at my third meeting. Suddenly it felt as if the cotton wool had been taken out of my ears and I could "hear" what everyone in the meeting was talking about for the first time and could truly identify, at depth, that I was indeed an alcoholic and needed help. I surrendered to this fact completely, without reservation at that meeting and as I write this now I am 2 months away from my 20th clean and sober birthday. 20 years without anything in my system stronger than a paracetamol.

Chapter 5

Layer Upon Layer

What I see now looking back at my early recovery is that life felt very raw. My emotions, which I buried very deeply from the age of 4, began to surface. I never saw myself as an angry person, but that is exactly what I felt most of the time in those early months. I was angry at God, at myself, at my parents and the world. How could I, with my intellect and skills end up penniless, in a council house with two young children and no way out. The mountain in front of me seemed once more insurmountable. I continued to go to my meeting once a week as I could not afford a babysitter more than that but even that one meeting a week helped enormously. I also continued to see the counsellor, which also helped. He offered me the opportunity to go in to the treatment centre for 6 weeks, but I did not want to leave my children. I remember many evenings pacing back and forth in my living room once the children had gone to bed feeling like a caged animal. I kept hearing "one day at a time," (or one minute at a time if needed)", "keep coming back", and "don't pick up the first drink, if you don't pick up the first drink you can't get drunk". All these platitudes made great sense and the one that helped me the most was "let go and let God" which I repeated over and over as my mantra. Every time I thought about a drink I would replace it with my mantra. I completely avoided spending time with anyone I had drunk with previously and I did not go to wet places, or parties at all in those early days. I felt very lonely, vulnerable, ill at ease, and my nerve endings were raw. I did what I had to do to get through each day without picking up a drink, I cleaned my house, took the children to the park if it was nice, cooked, ate and, after the first week, slept better than I had done in many years.

My recovery began on 5th January 1997. In the October of 1996 I had started a degree course in music. I focused on this as much as I could as my mind cleared. Then something happened that happens to so many in early sobriety. I met someone in the rooms of AA who was nearly a year sober. He seemed like a God to me. He could quote chapter and verse from the literature. He had been through a 12-step treatment centre and moved to live with his aunt, just outside of the Shire. My love addiction kicked in. I now know that I merely switched addictions, from booze to love, but at the time he seemed like the answer to all my prayers. Within 18 months he had moved in and within 2 years we got married. This was even though he had relapsed just after making it to a year, even though he was also a heroin addict and not just an alcoholic and even though as soon as he moved in to live with us when we got engaged, his behavior was completely off the wall. He would keep me up night after night accusing me of all sorts, that someone fancied me, or that I had spoken to another male at a meeting. It was total insanity. I have no idea how I kept going and how I managed to finish my degree. The counsellor kept telling me "you need this man like you need a hole in the head", but I couldn't hear him, my needing to attach and love addiction were stronger for me than any drink or drug I had ever imbibed. It was right in the core of me like a stick of rock. I stopped seeing the counsellor.

After we were married life gradually settled down as we both worked through the 12 steps of recovery. After finishing my degree, I was offered a part time lecturer's position, teaching at the university where I had trained, running a community choir and working with a PHD student as a drummer on a new module they were offering. I really wanted to say yes, it was what my heart dreamt of and why I had started to do the degree in the first place, but my husband said no, you need a full time job, so without any fight on my part whatsoever I gave up on my dream, just as I had when my first boyfriend asked me not to go to university when I was 18. Instead I got my first job as a deputy manager at a day centre for adults with severe learning difficulties. My husband worked for a small building company and we bought our first house together. The children were happy, especially my son as we would all go out cycling or walking in nature and bought a cheap caravan so we could go caravanning most weekends whenever the weather was good. For the first time in my life I felt safe, secure, happy. I liked being married and saying, "my husband this or that" to the other women at work. I felt like I was a part of life, like I belonged and was "normal". I had a husband, a job, a degree, a mortgage, a car and two children that I loved. My husband was 6 years younger than me and really adored me. After we got married his mood swings were a lot less, as was his paranoia and we were relatively happy together. He was not violent; he was a gentle soul who loved being part of a family. I got on well with his family, and he got on well with mine. Like all relationships there were difficulties, but nothing that threatened our happiness or stability.

We sold our first house and bought a much bigger house slightly further out of town with a fantastic garden. He was now training to be a precision engineer, working long hours and studying hard. My job was going well until at 4 ½ years sober I injured my back and couldn't work for 6 months. I thought I would never work again. I was in constant pain. I became very depressed, as it was hard to even lift my arm the pain was so excruciating. I didn't want to drink but wasn't sure if I wanted to live. I really couldn't see a way forward. I couldn't take strong painkillers as I knew I would get addicted to anything with Codeine in it, Ibuprofen made me feel weird and paracetamol just didn't touch the pain. My husband became very fearful about our financial future and started to work double shifts. I hardly saw him. He would get up before I was awake and get home after I had gone to bed. His caffeine intake went through the roof and he started to get horrific headaches. I pleaded with him to stop, but he could not hear me, all he could hear was his own fear. Our marriage began to falter. When I did see him he was angry, tired, in pain, sensitive to light and totally intolerant of any noise, so the children, who had been a great source of joy for him, became a real nuisance, and had to be kept out of his way as much as possible. I later found out that alongside the caffeine he had also started to abuse codeine. He eventually had to have two sinus operations and was signed off work. He failed to tell the nurse that he was a recovering addict after the first operation and was given morphine-based drugs for the pain. When he got out of the hospital he continued to take codeine secretly. This was the beginning of the end for us

.

I had to go and look for a job to keep us afloat. I saw an advert for a self-employed insurance agent. I knew I could walk and talk, I could not sit at a desk all day because of my back and there were absolutely no jobs for a musician, so insurance it had to be. Although I was good at it, there were days when I literally could not get out of the door to go and trawl around industrial units looking for self-employed people to sell the product to (it was income protection). I would either not leave the house or leave but go and sit in my car somewhere away from the house for hours on end until I would eventually give in and return home defeated and dejected. At the time I just thought it was extreme shyness or that it was fear masquerading as procrastination. I now know it was part of my love addiction. The part of me which surfaces from time to time and is totally and overwhelmingly debilitating; it has been present to one degree or another throughout my whole life, but it wasn't until I looked at my love addiction later that I began to understand it. It is the inability to feel part of a group, to always feel like the outsider, to be completely unable to be around groups of people of any description, whether through work or in social situations. It is not just a lack of confidence, extreme shyness or anxiety; it is a total inability to be around any group of people whatsoever. There were always times when I could "act as if" and put on the amour and go and do battle with the demon in my head who told me "you can't", "you are not worthy" and the worst one "you are invisible". Yet on the days when my negative head won, no amount of "acting as if" could make it possible for me to be around people. I do not know if this stems from the childhood abuse, the resultant shame or some other reason and in a way, it does not matter, all I know is that it has always been present to a greater or lesser degree, it was one of the reasons I drank and took drugs and without those in my life to mask the feelings, it returned with a vengeance.

Eventually I moved on to another more well know insurance company and really started to do well. I built a large book of business and felt it was time to let my husband follow his dream of starting his own business. His headaches had ceased, and he appeared to be back to normal. He set up a business in the building trade and both of us were earning decent money, the house we had bought was looking good, the children were holidayed at least twice a year, indeed I took nearly every August off to spend with them. Life was easier now that we had both been sober a while, it was calmer, we had no money worries to speak of, all our bills were paid, we had two vehicles, but I felt empty inside. I did not sing or go to concerts or festivals any more. It felt like I had painted myself into a wardrobe in recovery, where my life was all about work, meetings and family, but I was not to be found anywhere. The creative me, the alternative me, the free spirited me was buried deep. It was as though I had sold myself for a vision of normality that began to turn to ashes in my mouth and choke me bit by bit. I loved my husband and children very much but hated my work and I felt like I was dying inside. I began to pull away from my husband emotionally and physically and I was too busy doing this to notice his behavior change. It is only in hindsight that I can see that he drank ridiculous amounts of caffeine yet was able to fall asleep easily. He became more secretive and less wanting to spend time with the children. His mood swings returned and got worse until one day he threw out my son's snooker table because he was laughing whilst he was playing a game on it. That woke me up again and I realized something had to change, his behavior was not OK. He admitted he had been misusing Codeine all this time and that that explained his behavior. I felt like there was also something else he was withholding from me but did not know what it was. I asked him to leave and sort himself out.

My husband rented a room around the corner from me in a lady's house and we went to couples counseling, which really did not help at all. One day a voice from nowhere said to me to walk round and see if his van was where he was staying, it was not, and I suddenly knew he had been having an affair with one of my friends and that was where he was. I went back home and drove around there. Sure enough his van was parked around the corner from her house. I rang him up and confronted him, he said he was working at a different house in the same area, so I drove back around to where he said he had been working and knocked on the door. The man was at home, so I made up an excuse about my husband leaving some tools there when he last worked there. Of course, he said there were no tools and my husband finished the job a month ago. I thanked him and left. Every single part of me wanted to scream and go around to her house and confront her, punch her lights out, kneecap him, generally just do one or both physical harm. Instead I drove back home screaming expletives whilst driving and went into my kitchen and exploded. A sound came out of me like an injured wild animal. I felt like I could not breathe. Tears were streaming down my face. The children were hugely concerned and confused, but I couldn't hold it together, not even for them. I was so incredibly hurt. I felt I had been betrayed by my best friend and by a woman I had been helping every week for 2 years as a mentor. It was the most excruciating emotional pain I had ever felt up to that point. I could no longer deaden my emotions with booze, drugs or a man and boy did it hurt. I rang him and screamed that I wanted a divorce and to get his things out of my house. He denied the whole thing, but she admitted it. I knew I could never trust or have him anywhere near me again. Our marriage was shattered into 1000 pieces and so was my heart.

He started drinking, smoking weed and eventually went back to heroin use. He would turn up at my door in all sorts of states. I held firm. Then one day my love addiction kicked back in. I decided I would try again. No sane person would have re-engaged with a using addict at this point, especially with my first-hand knowledge of the chaos and destruction that goes on in the families of active addicts. I was out the other side and thought it was a good idea to go back in and "dance with the drug". Whilst heroin was his drug of choice, he was mine. I don't know if it was my pride, that I didn't want the other woman to have him, or just addiction that I didn't want to live without him, but to walk back into the chaos knowingly can only be described as insanity, masquerading as love addiction. At the time though I couldn't see it. A good friend of mine told me I was being very foolish, but I wouldn't listen. I thankfully kept him away from the children and would go and see him at the place he lived, rather than at our house. The other woman would sometimes turn up outside and start shouting. On one occasion the paramedics had to be called as he had almost od'd and at one point I was in the car with him driving erratically. I screamed at him to stop the car and got out and walked back home. It was total chaos, but it kept me from the pain of facing the feelings about the betrayal and my failed marriage. Then one day it was as if my sanity returned. I could detach again and knew that the only solution right now was divorce, as my children could have ended up parentless. I was putting my life at risk for the sake of a fix of his company, the quality of which was soul destroyingly awful. I somehow managed to break contact with him again, no calls, texts, seeing or speaking to him whatsoever. I knew this was the only way for me to get him out of my system; "cold turkey" was what had to happen whether it was alcohol, heroin or love addiction.

I started divorce proceedings and came up with an offer I thought was fair. He accepted the offer and we went our separate ways. Needless to say, it did not last long with the "other woman", he moved out of the area and I was left to deal with the mess. My daughter had never really got on with him, she found him too controlling, so she was relieved more than anything that he was no longer in our life, but my son was devastated. He had formed a real attachment to my first husband and as he was in his mid-teens he was very deeply affected. Almost overnight he stopped playing football and began making music. At the same time, he started drinking, smoking weed and taking drugs. I felt powerless to help him as I was on my knees emotionally and had nothing left to give.

At this point I it had been 10 years since my last drink and yet I felt at my absolute emotional rock bottom. I realized that I did not have any close female friends that I felt really connected to who could help me get through this period. I had made my husband the centre of my universe and everything else had fallen away apart from my AA recovery. I could no longer get what I needed from my local Alcohol Anonymous meetings as I felt unsupported and judged, so I started attending other meetings for people who have a problem with drugs (Narcotics Anonymous) which helped enormously. I also started seeing a new therapist who kept telling me that I was a love addict and needed to get to attend a group that dealt with this issue (Sex and Love Addicts Anonymous). I really did not see myself as a sex addict or as having a problem with sex whatsoever but could identify completely with being a love addict. I knew deep down that I would not make it in my recovery from booze if I did not address my issues around relationships. My failed marriage had taken me to my emotional rock bottom.

There were no local meetings dealing with love addiction, so I found a couple of women in Narcotics Anonymous who were also interested in attending a recovery meeting for relationship issues and we drove up to a few meetings in London. It was about a 6-hour round trip but was totally worth it. I heard women talking about obsession, compulsion, acting in and out, promiscuity and sexual anorexia. I heard them talking about multiple failed relationships with addicts and alcoholics, of being born into dysfunctional families and of having lived in families where sexual or physical abuse had been present. I heard about careers that had never gotten off the ground and about losing oneself in another person. I heard so many things that made utter sense. There was a level of sharing here that I had never experienced in any other fellowship prior to this. When I returned to the counsellor and told him how brilliant it was to get to the SLAA meetings, he encouraged me to start a local group. I resisted for about 3 months and then relented. I started women only meeting in my hometown. The two original women came, and others soon joined us. That meeting is still going 10 years later. There are now 4 local meetings a week in that town. I found a woman in another part of the Shire who could take me through the steps. I then took others through them, who then took others and there are now many recovering men and women who have worked through these steps and into a better life.

I do believe attending that SLAA meeting saved my life. It helped me look at my relationship issues, which had been a problem for me before I ever picked up a mood-altering substance. As a child I had lived in fantasy from when my abuse occurred. I recognized that from the point of the abuse a part of me had split off from myself and had never returned. From the age of four I felt as though I was watching a video of my life rather than being present in it. The drink, drugs and relationships were all just coping mechanisms, ways to distract me from my ever-present soul sickness. There were many tears, much laughter and strong bonds of true friendship forged in the women's group that are still present today. I learned that one of the ways my love addiction showed up most in my life was in my relation to other people. I learned about "social anorexia" a term used to describe people, like me, who felt apart from and isolated from pretty much everyone else on the planet. I learned about having walls or absolutely no boundaries at all, both symptoms of love addiction and a poor substitute for having healthy boundaries. I learned that I was sexually anorectic, that without drink or drugs inside me I was unable to fully connect on an intimate level. I realized that I was absolutely terrified of real intimacy, not just with partners, but also with friends, family and even my children. I did not know who I was and one of my biggest fears was that if I stripped away all the layers you would find nothing there, I would just be the "hole in the donut".

Chapter 6

Melting of the Heart

The next couple of years were all about defrosting my heart and feeling my feelings. My friendships grew until I felt "part of". I will always be grateful to my first fellowships for getting me into recovery and helping me to stay away from mood altering substances, which was an absolutely necessary prerequisite for the work I have done in SLAA. However, what I now know is that true recovery for me could not happen until I made the journey from my head to my heart and for that to happen I had to feel safe enough and held by my higher power and the other women in this fellowship. My self-esteem began to grow, as did my self-care and self-love. I realized that even though I had been in several long-term, committed, relationships I had never fully let anyone in. Once the first flush of "new love" had worn off, my sexual and emotional anorexia would resurface, and the relationship would deteriorate. I would feel increasingly like I was suffocating and would pull away emotionally. I also realized I subconsciously chose other emotionally unavailable, "damaged" partners who were also unable to connect on an emotional level and would therefore not challenge my anorectic core. Not all my partners were emotionally unavailable, my first love was emotionally present and available, which is why I had to wreck the relationship. He wanted "normal" and whole, which I just couldn't do.

Most of my relationships were battlegrounds for my fear of intimacy to play itself out on. I would oscillate between my need to feel in control of a relationship, or other person, and unhealthy dependency upon that person (co-dependency). My relationships were very rarely adult-to-adult; they were usually child-to-child, or critical parent-to-child where I switched between the critical parent role and the helpless "save me" child role. The next few years were about forming true relationships with others where I learned to relate from my adult self as much as possible, and, when appropriate, I could allow my inner child to come out and play. I learned how to deal with conflict more effectively. In most of my friendships before attending SLAA I either never spoke my truth and was therefore inauthentic for fear of losing the friendship, or, on the rare occasion that I did speak my truth and thus enter into conflict, I would go into "black and white" thinking and would walk away from the relationship. I was incapable of working through the disagreement and therefore could not remain in the friendship. I did not know that the adult way was to work through the disagreement and in so doing strengthen the relationship. Along with "black and white" thinking was "magical thinking" which I had applied throughout my life about all my relationships. "Magical thinking" runs along the lines of assigning magical qualities to people and then when they do not live up to those totally unrealistic expectations, punishing them for it or just backing away completely and shutting the relationship down.

I began to learn that in adult relationships there is give and take, no one, including me, is perfect, and there is such a thing as "good enough". I also started to experience emotional balance, where I was not so much of a slave to my emotions. I learned that my emotional anorexia was my way of coping with my underdeveloped emotional core. It was not a good way, one that allowed me to grow, but it was an effective way of dealing with my terror of intimacy. How could I let another truly see me when I could not see myself? How could I love or be loved by another when I did not love and accept myself? It was not just that I did not trust myself, which I didn't, but that I did not know myself at all. I had taken substances for 10 years to hide that fact from myself and in my 10 years of recovery had switched from substances to my love addiction so that I still did not have to face this fact. I was terrified to sit with me, because without the drama and "other" there was no me. In SLAA I learned to just sit with me, with an emotion or a feeling. I had always believed that as soon as I felt something I had to "do" something about it. It was a revelation to me to learn that I could acknowledge and feel my feelings, then let the emotion go without it having to ruin my day or upset those around me. I made very slow progress but progress, not perfection, was the goal.

After a couple of years of thawing out my sexual and social anorexia flipped into "acting out", which was triggered by the increasing ill health and subsequent death of my Mother. I had learned that promiscuity and sexual anorexia are flip sides of the same coin. Whether acting out or acting in, the level of intimacy remains the same; zero. Most sex addicts are terrified of intimacy, the connection is purely physical, not emotional and the number of partners is a symptom of their fear of intimacy, not a means by which to address it. I started Internet dating and my addiction took off. I ended up on 4 different sites, speaking to many different men at once, thinking I was looking for a partner, but knowing that what I really wanted was physical closeness. I did not know how to be friends with men; it was just something I had never learned. I was either in a committed relationship with a man or they simply did not exist. After meeting several different men, I started dating one who lived about 200 miles away, which was perfect for my anorexia, but allowed me to get my "fix" when I wanted it. His name was Phil. I knew he was a sex addict, a liar and a cheat, but I was desperate to be held. When my Mum's health deteriorated still further my need to be "held" grew exponentially. I put myself into several dangerous situations. I continued to have trouble feeling my feelings and knew only how to act out or act in. I was acting out big style and would forgo work to drive and see him. He had no money, did not work and had had a breakdown after his business collapsed. We were totally unsuited to each other. I also knew he saw other women, sexually as well as socially, but when he denied it I pretended to believe him and carry on with the relationship. Sometimes I would drive all the way to see him and he would ignore me or be on the Internet speaking to other women. My self-esteem really suffered, and I felt like I was going insane. I have heard recovering alcoholics say the worse place to be is a head full of recovery and a belly full of beer, I felt the same way about the situation I was in. I could not understand with all the work I had done on myself throughout the years why I was yet again engaged in an emotionally abusive relationship. It did not make sense at the time, only with hindsight I now understand how causing myself emotional pain with him was my way to distract myself from the emotional pain around losing my mother, pain that I did not want to feel. This was not a conscious choice; it was unconscious and was merely my default position of masking my true feelings. The place where I used to live constantly was now a place I visited occasionally when under extreme emotional stress.

I was with him one night when I heard the news that my mother had died, and he did hold me through my tears, but I put myself through hell just for that moment. What I realize now is that all the drama and acting out was just my way of coping with my mum's death. I did not want to feel or know how to feel these feelings, they felt too big, like I was going to be completely overwhelmed and engulfed by them, that if I went in there to feel them I would never come back out. My relationship with my mother was complicated. Growing up I was terrified of upsetting her and would go out of my way to conform to her version of me. I felt loved and understood by her to an extent, but she had unresolved issues of her own. My fear of abandonment around her was at the core of my love addiction. It took me until I was 38 years old and 2 years sober to stand up to her and say "no". Even then it felt like I was going to die if she rejected me. I didn't die and even though she punished me for standing up to her, we grew closer because of it and our relationship improved enormously. I am grateful for the time I did have with her in my AA recovery.

The fear of abandonment is one of the reasons love addicts stay in and return to abusive relationships. There is no lonelier place in the world than to be in a relationship with someone who is emotionally unavailable, yet the love addict will stay there year after year, receiving nothing other than a few moments where the abuser is begging and pleading for you to take them back and for that short period you feel powerful and in control, wanted and needed. I was once asked to draw a picture of how I felt. I drew a desert with a tree dying from lack of water and a few drops of blood falling from the sky. Living with love addiction is very painful. It makes no sense, there is no big "payoff", there is a lifetime of starvation from love and a few moments of ecstasy, which turn to poison in a very short time. Every time I got in the car to drive and see Phil I hated myself even more. I knew it would be awful but told myself "this time it will be different, this time he will be loving and fun to be with". He never was, and it never was better it was worse each time. I love the definition of insanity "keep doing the same thing and expecting a different outcome". I ended the relationship shortly after my Mum died. I felt like I was in a constant fog. I was unable to do much work, but was financially OK for a few months, as I had sold some shares in a company I had helped to start. Rather than taking time out to grieve I went back on one of the dating sites and dated a couple of other guys, one of whom was grossly overweight, drank like a fish and smoked dope as often as he could. He did work, lived a long way away again and was very emotionally immature. I went away for the weekend with him to Bournemouth. The first night we were there he left me most of the night on my own whilst he "did the rounds" without me. When I tried to talk to him about it the following day when he was sober he just got angry and pulled away even more. The second night we were standing together at the start of the night when a group of women he knew stopped to talk to him (he was well known on the "circuit"). He turned to me as if he was going to invite me in to talk to them with him and instead asked me to pass him his camera, so they could all have a picture taken together. I felt humiliated and shamed, so grabbed my bag, went back to the hotel, packed my things and drove home. I left him a very emotional message on his phone, full of expletives and never saw him again.

Chapter 7

Even More Growth!

There had been another man on one of the sites who had pursued me just after I had met Phil. He was 10 years older than me, I did not fancy him at all, but felt like he would be a safe harbor for a while, so I got back in contact with him. When he originally contacted me, I had just started seeing Phil, so we never met up and I came off the site. This time we were both free to meet. He sounded genuinely pleased to hear from me. We spoke on the Monday and he promised to come and get me on Friday as he was working away at the time. He sounded sweet and caring as I explained to him what had happened in Bournemouth. He also recanted a tale of a woman he had seen for a while who had started stalking him. He turned up on Friday at the correct time where we had agreed to meet, in a public place, wearing a suit, which I am a sucker for. We went to a restaurant for a meal. We both liked music; a friend of mine at a music festival took the picture of me that was on my profile on the dating site, so that was a good start. He was charming, intelligent, attentive and extremely flattering. He behaved like a perfect gentleman. He did talk about himself a lot and was very confident, but I just put that down to his age and the fact that he had lived an interesting life.

He told me he had been married 3 times before, which rang alarm bells, but I ignored them. It felt good to be in conversation with a "grown up", he did not display any emotional insecurity and was not an alcoholic or drug addict, so they were all plus points. However, my alarm bells went off when we kissed goodnight. It was the worst kiss I had ever had. It felt like I was being invaded, not caressed and it really put me off. However, I felt bowled over by his keenness, he wanted to see me the next day, couldn't wait for me to meet his 30-year-old daughter and grandchildren who currently lived with him in another part of the Shire and so began another relationship. He really pushed the relationship on fast, wanted to take me away for the weekend within the first month of knowing him. He was very keen to get me to commit fully to the relationship. I kept putting the brakes on as much as possible as I really wanted to take things slower and really get to know him before I committed fully to him, but he just kept pushing, so of course I relented and 3 weeks into the relationship he took me and my dog away to the country to a lovely cottage for the weekend. I kept my boundaries in place on the Saturday night, but gave in on the Sunday. It was an OK experience, he was attentive to my needs, which was a relief, but I still did not like kissing him. It turned out that we had both lost the parent we were closest to that year and we were both grieving. He had also gone through divorce the same year and lost custody of his 11-year-old daughter, which he was far more upset about losing than his 3rd wife. He got pretty upset at one point talking about the loss of his father and I was able to hug him, so it felt like we were emotionally connecting as well as physically connecting.

I had started a life-coaching course with part of the money I got from the shares I sold. I was really enjoying it; the tutors were great and so were the other people on the course. I had studied NLP (Neuro Linguistic Programming[1]) previously so it felt like a natural progression. When I told him that I was going away in a couple of weeks for the weekend to attend my course, he suggested he come with me. He would stay in the hotel and work whilst I attended the course and then we could go out in the evening. It was about 5 weeks after we had first met, and as my birthday was approaching he said we would celebrate that too. The course was near Exeter, so we went a day earlier, and he bought me a guitar

---

[1] Neuro Linguistic Programming

from a shop for my birthday present. He also bought himself a new guitar at the same time. I was completely bowled over as I felt he really "got me" as a human being. I had had a previous boyfriend brake my guitar before, never buy me one. The fact that his new guitar cost a lot more than mine never entered my head. It did however feel wrong that he came with me that weekend, as the course was something I was doing for me and the fact that he was back at the hotel meant I couldn't go out that evening with my fellow students, which felt wrong.

It wasn't long before he wanted to spend every possible moment together, every evening and all my weekends were suddenly full of "us". I was unaware of what was happening, that I had actually met a man who was "love bombing" me, a term used to describe the attempt to accelerate the birth and growth of feelings within a relationship quickly by creating an intense atmosphere of affection and adoration, which is designed to disarm the other persons natural guardedness so that they do not question the direction and speed the relationship is headed in. I felt confused and tricked into believing that I was "the one", he actually said I was his "twin flame", bombarded me with compliments about every aspect of my personality and looks, told me how grateful he was to have found me, that he was "punching above his weight" and that because I did not drink I was nothing like his past wives who had all been big drinkers and had all cheated on him. Another aspect of the love bombing was dependency. He tried to make me dependent on him for all my needs. I was still vulnerable due to the death of my Mum, so I fell for it hook line and sinker. I never had time to see friends and went to less and less recovery meetings. He also began to denigrate the course I was on telling me I needed to go get a real job, so I did.

I went back to insurance for a while, even though I absolutely hated it. Part of my training was in London and of course he came with me to the hotel, to be supportive! I look back now and can see all the signs that I was being manipulated and controlled, but I was unaware of it then. Eight months after we met I did not recognize myself. I had been appointed a business development director for a large international firm, was driving his sports car, which he had given me, was earning nearly £100,000 a year, working 12-14-hour days and I was miserable. I was tired and irritable all the time, and spent my weekends catching up with shopping, cleaning and seeing his daughters or grandchildren. If I went to one recovery meeting a week

I was lucky. He had managed to mold me into exactly who he wanted me to be and in the process, I had lost me. He proposed to me, I accepted, and we got married 22 months after meeting each other. I still had absolutely no idea who he really was. My friends and family that had met him always said what a charming man he was and how attentive he was towards me. When I look at pictures that were taken from this time of the both of us, in every picture he is devouring me with his eyes, he is not looking at the camera, he is watching me.

There were a few instances that made me question our relationship. The first was on our second boxing day together. We were at my house and had arranged to travel to see my family. My father, both my sisters and respective husbands and two of my nieces were going to be there. We had arranged to be there for 1pm as my father had to eat regularly as an operation had left him with only half a stomach. By the time we got up and had a cooked breakfast it was time go, as it was a two-and-a-half-hour drive. He wanted to go and buy some new trousers in the Boxing Day sales, but I said no, we had to leave. We had a minor altercation in the house but when we got into the car he went ballistic. For nearly the whole journey he ranted, raved and smashed his hand down on the dashboard. I laughed in the beginning, thinking he would just get over it, it seemed like such a small thing to me, but he didn't get over it, he went on and on. By the time we got to my sisters I was in tears, white as a sheet, totally drained and not talking to him. The minute we walked through the door he put on his smile, entertained and charmed everyone, whilst I was quiet the whole time we were there. My family quizzed me on what was the matter and I just said it was work, that I was exhausted, so we ate, made our excuses and left early. I drove him to his house without saying a word the whole journey. I was supposed to be staying with him at his house, but instead I kept the engine running and drove off. I did not speak to him for several days, and when he turned up a few days later, he just pretended nothing whatsoever was wrong. I pulled him up on his behavior and said in no uncertain terms would I accept such behavior ever again, that if he ever acted in that way again I would ask him to go and we would be over. He did not acknowledge his behavior, nor apologize for it; he was just extra attentive and nice to me until I thawed out again.

All my warning bells were ringing, but my love addiction once more took over and I ignored my own truth. He did not like me saying "no" to him about

going shopping, I threatened his authority, so he ranted and raved until I was absolutely shattered emotionally and mentally exhausted from the 21/2-hour tirade. He could not own his part in the day, preferring only to say that it was my fault for not letting him get the trousers. There
was absolutely no way to make him understand how extreme his behavior was and how unacceptable it was, it was like talking to a brick wall, nothing could get through to him. I did pull back and have doubts, but of course by this time I was fully hooked and committed to the relationship. If I were not a love addict I would have run for the hills at this point. All my knowledge and work on myself just seemed woefully inadequate in overcoming my need to stay attached. My love addiction kept me there, hoping it was a one off, preferring to believe that the "good" far outweighed the "bad"

The next time something similar happened was after his youngest daughter's birthday party. We had all gone go-karting and had a competition to see who did the fastest round and who won the competition overall. When everyone's results came out saying I had won on both counts he and his oldest daughters partner said it was wrong and that one of them had in fact won. I let it go but a couple of weeks later we were camping with his youngest in Devon and had gone out for a bite to eat. He brought it back up, how ridiculous it was and how of course I was incapable of doing such a thing, he went on and on for about an hour in the restaurant. I tried reasoning with him, ignoring him, joining him in the argument, but nothing worked. He would not stick to the subject matter and would instead bring up every flaw and weakness in my personality and life that he could think of. Apart from the fact it was totally humiliating in the restaurant, especially in front of his daughter, it was also embarrassing and hugely painful. I dropped them off at the campsite and drove home, I was supposed to be staying, but could not stand to be anywhere near him. I left them to it the rest of the holiday and told him he needed to apologize to me and his daughter and that I would not continue with the marriage if he did not come to couples counseling with me. He refused but upped the ante on the attention front, showered me with "love" and affection, made me feel special and wanted and of course I let it slide.

He had always wanted to retire abroad, so we started planning for him to retire, sell both our houses, buy one abroad and one in the UK to rent out. I had stopped working full time the month after we got married in September 2013 through extreme stress. I realize now it was not just the job, although the long hours had taken their toll, it was the relationship that was the most draining. My head and heart were at war with each other. My heart wanted to believe in the fairytale that I had met my soul mate, my twin flame, and my life partner. My head kept telling me that there was something wrong with our relationship, the facts, when I dared to look at them, told me there was something not OK with my new husband, that I should never have married him, and I would be a fool to move abroad with him. I did not know what was wrong, but if I had known what I was really dealing with I would have run for my life. Whilst he was still working I got both houses ready to sell. Part of getting his house ready to sell was clearing out all his rubbish. It took 5 skips so was a big job. When I asked him why his oldest daughter was not helping, as a lot of the rubbish was hers or her children's, we had another massive argument. I simply could not fathom why he could not just ring her up and ask her to help, which I was sure she would have been happy to do. He just got angrier, put his hand up to say stop and refused to discuss the situation. I got back in my car, drove home and did not hear from him for a whole week, not one text, email, or message. I felt utterly devastated and extremely concerned that he could punish me in this way for daring to disagree with him again. I began to be terrified at the prospect of moving abroad with him, being completely at his mercy, isolated from my friends, family and support system. This time when he came back to see me, again without an apology, blaming his daughter for causing an argument between us, I insisted on couples counseling. He initially refused once more saying "people in my family don't talk to strangers about our matters", but relented when I said, "I will not go abroad with you unless we get help and find strategies for dealing with conflict in our marriage that do not involve you ranting and raving at me, denying my reality, or completely cutting me off for a whole week". This time I meant it as all my warning bells were going off in my head.

He came to one session and refused to go back but agreed that we would each write a contract of how we would treat each other. He never wrote anything down, and I went back to preparing both houses whilst he worked long hours. It reminded me very much of the relationship with my children's father. It was abusive, I knew I was not happy and wanted to get out but was unable to do so. Back then I could blame it on drink and drugs, now there was no such excuse. It was my love addiction and my co-dependency[2]. I did go back to

---

[2] Co-Dependency

working part time in insurance again before we moved abroad as I did not like being financially dependent on him as it gave him too much power within the relationship but moving abroad meant that I would be totally dependent on his pensions. The idea was that we would start playing music together and earn money that way as well as look at setting up businesses once we were over there.

We had bought a house abroad with the proceeds of his house that was very remote, it had no neighbours, the nearest village was a half hour perilous walk and the nearest town was a 40-minute drive away. The idea was that we would have the space to think and be able to make as much noise as we wanted. It was also off-grid, ran on solar and wind power, had no mains gas or electric and had a water tank that had to have water delivered to it by a tanker. It was a full-time job for him just trying to get it all to work. I did my best to help, cut off dead branches from the hundreds of almond trees on our land, dislocated my clavicle moving stones outside the front of the house, did all the cooking, shopping and cleaning and started playing the guitar in earnest after a 30-year break (apart from the odd tinkle). Within a short time of being there the arguments started. I had done a blog on our journey of the drive from the UK, which lots of people read and said they enjoyed. He pulled it apart and said all I did was make fun of him, which was true only to a point, as I made fun of myself even more. He was incapable of laughing at himself and became very angry and aggressive at the thought of other people laughing at him. He told me he would never read anything of mine again, so I stopped writing. When we started playing music together he would pull me up all the time about my guitar playing but hated the fact that I could play reggae and he couldn't. He started to pull apart my singing, and whilst I am not the "best" singer in the world, I know my instrument and others like it for its warmth and expression. There began to be a marked disconnect with what he said to me and how he talked about me to other people. He would always sing my praises to others but was totally different behind closed doors. I was freaked out at being abroad, homesick, worried about my children (they were in their mid-20's but had been living at home until just before we left), not getting to enough meetings or meeting enough new people. Instead of understanding this he just got more and more angry and verbally abusive towards me. When our car stopped working and the only way to get anywhere was in the now illegal van, (which he had lost the key for on the day we were leaving to go to the ferry), which I could not even start, as you had to go through a 10 minute procedure in order to make the only surviving key work and regardless of how many times I tried it, I could only get it to work one time in about 100, whilst he could do it about 1 in every 2 attempts. I could therefore not get to my recovery meetings and when he refused to take me anywhere, as he was "busy" I flipped, grabbed a bag and walked. All I knew was I had to get out. I felt like something bad was going to happen as the frequency and the intensity of the arguments were escalating. He told me I needed to go have a drink, which, after 18 years of sobriety was an awful thing to say. It felt like my sobriety, my sanity and ultimately my life was in jeopardy.

I went down to the coast to look at a property that I was thinking of buying with the proceeds of my house and when it was time to return I burst into tears. I just couldn't do it. I felt bereft and like I would literally die if I returned to the house and back to him. I had no clothes with me, just my handbag, so I walked to a local hotel and booked myself in for a few nights. A few nights turned into a week and then two weeks. I really could not face seeing or talking to him. I was hurt, incredibly angry, upset, devastated, missing my animals and did not have a clue what to do. I spent huge amounts of time on my own as I knew very few people, apart from a couple of people in recovery. The loneliness bit into me. It was like a cancer that ate at my soul. I went to three recovery meetings a week and one women in recovery meeting and had the occasional coffee with kind members, but that still left most of my week unstructured and unfilled. Time hung heavy on me and I was tempted to contact him, but I didn't. I decided instead to look for somewhere to rent. Everyone said that I wouldn't find anywhere until October, as everywhere would be rented out for hundreds of Euros a week as it was a coastal resort in August. I could not afford to stay any longer at the hotel and I really did not want to go back up to the isolation and arguments. I rang around all the local estate agents and each one said the same, nothing to rent until October. I tried one last one and they said a 3-bed house 5 minutes' walk from the beach was available from a few days' time for 6 months at 400 Euros a month, a phenomenally low figure for the coast, so I took it. I had no furniture, so someone sold me a sofa bed, I picked up a picnic table from the local ferreteria (DIY shop) and I bought cutlery and crockery, a few pans and a kettle from a second-hand shop. I had also been raiding the local charity shops for clothes, so had an odd assortment of things to wear, none of which fitted me properly, but I didn't care.

My life was simple. Get up early (4-5 am) go for a walk along the coast before it got too hot. Have breakfast about 9, catch a bus to do my food or clothes shopping, get to a meeting or meet a friend if possible, read, sit by the beach under an umbrella, swim if the water wasn't too choppy, rest on my sofa bed when it was too hot to do anything else, as the temperature was way in the high 30s and the humidity was horrendously high and just be. It was cooler and had lower humidity in the mountains where the house was situated, but I just couldn't go back. Most nights I couldn't get to sleep until gone midnight because of the heat, (no air conditioner). Other than fruit I couldn't eat anything between breakfast and about 7 at night, so I lost weight and through the sheer amount of sweating I did all day. I could have a cold shower and before I had even put my clothes on I was soaking again. Heat is one thing but dealing with the humidity was horrendous. I managed to get through all of August and was looking forward to it getting a bit cooler. Then my love addiction kicked in again. I was really through the worst bit but decided I needed to get my things and pick up my animals, as it was not fair on my husband or them that I had abandoned them at the house. I organized a lift with a couple I know and arranged it with my ex to go pick up my dog, two cats and some of my belongings. When I saw him, my heart went back into addiction mode. I gave him a hug and wished him well, but I felt very vulnerable seeing him again. I should have arranged for someone else to get my belongings.

The problem with love addiction is that any contact between you and your ex ignites your love addiction and sets the awful wheels in motion once again. This is why, in recovery from love addiction, it is necessary to set "bottom lines" which are behaviors that you will <u>not</u> engage in such as seeing or contacting your ex, and "top line" behaviors that help your life to improve. You must be aware that the addict in you wants to re-attach at any cost. It is no different than how an untreated alcoholic feels without a drink; at some point, however horrific the last drunk was, the thought that a drink will make things better will return. All the thoughts about the arguments, the fear, the degradation, the lowering of my self-esteem through an unending stream of belittling comments, the feeling of being controlled and mentally and emotionally abused left me, to be replaced by "how nice it would be to be in his arms again" and "this time it will be different, he's learned his lesson and he will treat me well from now on". To any outsider these thought based on fantasy and wishful thinking seem like insanity, but to the addict, they make perfect sense. I had been without my recovery meetings for too long, my old '" sick head" had returned, just as it did with my first husband, but this time there was no one there in recovery to point out to me how insane my thinking was. The reality was I was lonely and wanted to be part of "us "again, a small part of me knew it was a bad idea, but the larger part said I am not ready to give up on my marriage yet. That thought cost me a lot of money and peace of mind. I was a fool to myself and did not protect my future or my money, but this is typical love addict behavior.

Ironically, we had our loveliest Christmas together that year with his youngest daughter and the two of us, down in the house on the coast. We were on the beach on Christmas day and went for a lovely meal. However, our relationship soon deteriorated again and by mid-April I could take no more of the verbal, mental and emotional abuse. I intended to rent a property as the lease on the house at the coast was now finished but had to leave suddenly as it felt like he had upped the ante on the verbal abuse, so I went and stayed back in our house on my own with my animals. I spent the best part of 4 months there yet felt less isolated than when I lived there with him. The only grey points were whenever he would turn up and start verbally abusing me. I survived, and in certain ways, facing my fears of being alone in the countryside with no one around, fears around poverty, belonging, worth, shame around my second failed marriage, loneliness eating at me from the inside and practical fears around hurting myself and there being no one around who could help me. One day I woke up and knew I had to decide whether to live in fear or in faith, so I chose faith. After that decision it felt like I had entered a new dimension. I really got in touch with my creativity and an explosion of songs came out of me, my connection to spirit also deepened through meditation and because of my physical isolation I was forced into reaching out to people for help. Making myself vulnerable, asking for help, has always been one of my greatest challenges, but I had to do it to survive. During the four months I lived at the house on my own my father's health deteriorated and he eventually died. I did get to spend a couple of weeks with him in his last days. On the day I got back to the house after spending time with my ailing father, my husband turned up and started screaming at me that I should return to England, that no one wanted me here and that I was squatting in his house. As both properties were in both names I was certainly within my right to live there. He seemed completely unhinged. I later learned that at 66 years of age he had started seeing a 28-year-old, which might account for his behavior.

When I refused to leave our property, he upped the ante and told me I had to start paying him rent on both properties, which worried me greatly as I was living solely on the small rent from our property in the UK. When I got back from my father's funeral I found that he had changed the locks on my front door and put a huge padlock on the outside railings therefore completely barring me from entry to the property. I was very distraught about this but also angry. He wasn't living there himself, he just didn't want me to reside there out of spite and control. I went to the police station and recounted my tale. They were most unhelpful, and their only advice was "change the locks yourself" as they said legally the property was still in both names. I subsequently employed a locksmith at great expense and the lock was changed back. Two days later I went out for a couple of hours to a local market. When I returned from the market I found the property wide open, the door destroyed and my dog cowering in the corner. I again returned to the police station and once again they were most unhelpful. I stayed at a female friend's house for the night, as I did not feel safe enough to return to the house. My concern was that he could have returned to the house at any time and been able to walk right in, so I arranged for a friend of mine and myself to go back to the house early the following morning to retrieve some of my possessions. I put my dog in kennels, my few belongings that I had managed to salvage into storage, gave away my cats to a friend to look after permanently and returned to the UK to rent out a room from a friend whilst I started the divorce process.

My life was full of drama, fear and chaos just as it had been all those years before with the children's father and my first husband. I felt like a failure, ashamed at the depths of where my love addiction had once again taken me. I felt powerless over how I had ended up in such a bad state once again. I had spent years working on my love addiction and gained a lot of knowledge about my disease, but when it came to the crunch I realized that my addiction had not stood still, it had progressed and as I had failed to keep treating my disease with meetings and ongoing recovery work, it had returned with a vengeance. My love addiction, like any other addiction, had been waiting patiently in the wings, waiting to re-assert itself once I stopped attending meetings and working on my recovery. It was cunning, baffling, powerful and very patient. I see now that he was not the cause of all my pain, I was. I failed to listen to my own red flags, of which there were plenty. I allowed myself to be bamboozled into emotionally and physically connecting much faster than I wanted to. I didn't listen to myself when I told him I would not go abroad with him without us seeing a couple's counsellor. It was me that said yes when he asked me to marry him. It was me that knew what he was really like after the first instance in the car and I DID NOT LISTEN. I failed to behave like a love addict in recovery and behaved instead as an active love addict. I paid a very high price, not just in terms of money, although the house sale, hotel bills, rent for the property on the coast, the lump sum I gave him, and all my other expenses wiped me out financially; the real cost was my peace of mind, my serenity, my dreams and the peace of mind of my children, family and friends in and out of recovery. The energy that had gone into surviving the chaos could have been much better spent in building a future for myself. What I later learned is that my second husband was a narcissist, which is classed as a mental illness. Narcissists sole aim in life is to be adored, and they cannot take any view of life that differs from their own. They are incapable of self-reflection. I did the only thing possible when in a relationship with a narcissist – I got out.

Back in the UK I started attending both AA and SLAA meetings once again. I spoke openly and honestly about where my disease had taken me. I shed many tears and got in touch with a whole heap of emotions. I realized that I had not grieved over the death of my father at all as I had been too caught up in my chaos. I recognized that I had caused myself pain with a relationship to mask my pain of losing my remaining parent. In recovery we look for patterns of behavior, not just specific instances. What resonated with me was the truth around causing myself pain when I am in pain, one of my childhood coping strategies. Over the next 9 months, waiting for the divorce to finalize, I turned the corner again and returned to sanity. My months in the UK were educational and inspirational. I felt like I had once again really begun to get in touch with who I really am and make a commitment to myself to truly be all of me, to share with the world the real authentic me, hiding nothing, whether it is my brilliance or my flaws. I have committed to finishing this book, have ideas for two more and have recorded an album of 12 original songs, which I am very proud of. I am less than a month away from the final court case, have seen my ex out and about with his latest girlfriend and survived it. I felt sorry for him, but that is another story for another time.

In myself I now feel more secure in who I am. I am absolutely committed to making the world a better place by being all of me and sharing my message through songs, the written word and how I am in the world. I am back living abroad and have rented a property for a year. Even though I really dislike the extreme heat, I am enjoying being here and being in my own place once again, surrounded by friends, peace and calm. I made a conscious decision to live abroad again as I feel I owe it to myself to face my fear and make a success of my life here. If I choose to move on at any point in the future it will be a thoughtful decision, not a kneejerk reaction to being bullied.

I am not interested in looking for a "man" to make me feel better, as I know my energy and focus needs to be on building my new life. When I am ready I know the type of person I will attract will be very different from my last partner, as I will never again enter a relationship with anyone who is not self-aware, spiritually connected and emotionally mature. I know the area I need to grow in most is my own emotional maturity, as all addicts, whether in recovery from their addiction or still active within it, are emotionally immature. Whilst that is still true for me, I am however aware of it and work hard at "growing up". The more mindfulness I practice, meditation I do, creative visualization and end goal setting I do, the more I mature emotionally. I speak my truth with all who are in my life with loving-kindness and my boundaries are healthy and intact. The traits that hold most addicts back are low self-esteem, over sensitivity, self-absorption and selfishness, so I continue to work on these. Progress not perfection is the key. The added traits for the love addict are control, co-dependency, manipulation, fear of intimacy, isolation, failure to show up for one's own life, addiction to drama and giving one's power away. These I really am working hard on. I am showing up for my life and this book is proof of that.

After another 6 months of committing to myself to "show up" for my life I have been attending a yoga class, a spiritual development group, I have launched my album, in two countries, started a band and two duets, am writing songs again and finishing writing this book. I am happier in myself than I have been in a very long time; there is no drama in my own life. I lost some 'friendships' along the way, some dropped away naturally and others I consciously moved away from. I only have people in my life who are open, honest, self-aware and loving. I have been asked out twice and declined gracefully as I know I am nowhere near ready for another relationship. I need time to grow spiritually so that I become the best version of me and therefore attract a different kind of relationship. More important for me right now is my relationship with myself. Being in a relationship with "another" for me right now is nowhere near as important. My focus is on improving my own life financially, emotionally and spiritually.

Chapter 8

Stories from other Love Addicts

Jade

My love addiction started young, probably as young as 6 or 7 when I played kiss chase in the school playground. It sounds harmless, but I now know that I was craving attention and validation, a way for me to know that I was "good enough" as I felt far from "good enough" most of the time. From the outside my family of origin looked normal, but there was a lot of neglect, emotional neglect. We were well cared for regarding food, clothing, our home, toys and classes outside of school – dancing, swimming and such, but there was no discussion about feelings. It felt that having feelings or problems of any kind, was not "acceptable", so I learnt to stuff my feelings down in a variety of ways. I used food, exercise, craving attention and seeking validation from others (love addiction) and I was never still, always doing something. I was a human doing, not a human being (although not consciously), probably from as young as 4 or 5. As I got older alcohol became my first drug of choice, with sex & love addiction and food following closely on its heels.

I found it hard to make and keep friends. I always wanted to be someone's "best friend" but never felt that I was. I was lonely for a lot of my childhood and bullied when I was older for being different. I was very tall and well developed by the time I was 12. I had my first boyfriend at 13 but had had crushes throughout my childhood. Even in my first relationship, I was a compulsive people pleaser, allowing him to touch me in ways that I wasn't comfortable with so that he didn't dump me. I was so desperate to be loved, as I didn't feel loved by my parents, not in the way that I wanted to feel loved. Throughout my teens there were several boyfriends, although none over-lapping, it was more about having the next one in the wings to replace the current one when the "magic" stopped working as it inevitably did. By then it was just too painful to be alone, to not be part of a relationship, so I was always on the lookout for the next guy, who was going to fix the (lonely) hole in me.

Although there had been sexual touching and exploration, I was 16 before I lost my virginity, and my initial thoughts were "is that it"? We were both inexperienced and it really didn't do that much for me, but it became a tool for me to hook the next guy in, to ensure that I was never alone. From then on until my early 30's, I pretty much started every new relationship as a one-night stand. I did not always want to be sexual, but I felt that I had to. Basically, I was prostituting myself, without any exchange of cash, just to feel wanted. If I met someone who wasn't interested in sex on the first date I really didn't know how to handle the situation, I felt that I wasn't good enough, desirable enough, pretty enough, thin enough, ad infinitum. Wanting to be thin enough helped deepen my already burgeoning eating disorder, where I swung between under and over eating and compulsively exercising when I over-ate. I thought that if I were thin enough, surely someone would find me attractive and want to be in a relationship with me. I also dated people because they showed an interest in me, rather than because I was interested in them. However, I did get engaged when I was 21, but was way too young and the relationship didn't last. As always, I moved onto someone else straight after breaking off my engagement.

My alcoholism started to show itself in my mid 20's. I had stopped swimming competitively, so now had the opportunity to go out at weekends & party. OMG alcohol was my best friend. It allowed me to be the person I thought I should be, funny, seductive, likeable, and sexy. It allowed me to be even more sexual than I had been previously. It gave me courage! But it wasn't long before I was its slave and a daily drinker. I met my ex-husband when I was 25, moved in with him after only dating for 3 months and was engaged after just over 11 months. I thought my life was sorted, but in reality, it was cracking under the strain of my addictions. I realized on my honeymoon that I had made a mistake, I was in love with the idea of being married, and not actually in love with the man I had married. I became sexually anorexic (withdrawn from sexual and emotional intimacy) after the marriage, partly because as soon as we were married I felt as though I had become my husband's possession and partly because of my fear of intimacy. Skirts that were ok for me to wear for work before we were married were suddenly too short. I felt suffocated by him and the relationship, so I withdrew. Intimacy was terrifying for me, although I didn't learn this until much later. Allowing someone (my husband, partner or friend) to see the real me was never going to happen. One, I didn't know who I was because I was a master chameleon, being whatever I thought the person I was with wanted me to be so that I wouldn't be rejected and two, if they did see the real me they would find so much wrong with me they would reject me. It became normal for me to be drunk before I could have sex with my husband. At times it was incredibly painful (I had un-diagnosed endometriosis) but I never said anything because I didn't want to be rejected, even though it was ok for me to reject him - double standards!!! The Christmas following our marriage (7 months later) my husband bought me a ring, and as he gave it to me he said, "She'll have to love me now". I felt as though I was being bought and it made me withdraw even more. My drinking continued to increase as a way for me to deal with my feelings. It was my anesthetic. I was desperately unhappy, deep in my growing alcoholism, eating disorder, compulsive busyness and what I now know as co-dependent behavior patterns. I did what I had always done; I started looking for a "replacement" partner. None of these behaviors were done consciously, but the patterns were there and had been for a very long time.

I did leave my husband after 13 months of marriage, causing him to have a breakdown as he blamed me for taking away his opportunity to have his own children (he was 7yrs older than me and 35 when we split up). I went headlong straight into another relationship. Again, living together very soon after getting together, but this time there was an ex-wife & 2 small child as part of the package and I didn't have the skills or tools to deal with any of it. My growing alcoholism took a giant leap forwards and I became a daily drinker. My life just became more and more chaotic and complicated. There were many arguments around his ex-wife; I just couldn't understand why a mother would use her children to get back at her husband, whom she left for someone else. I was desperate to be a mother myself. This dysfunctional relationship lasted about 3 1/2 years and was also plagued by my sexual anorexia. I tried leaving him earlier than that, but he threatened to commit suicide. He was a display pilot and he threatened to fly his aircraft into the side of a hill. I quickly backtracked, convinced him that he should buy a house for us to live in, by now his divorce had been settled and he was free to do what he wanted. When the house went through I went through the motions of decorating and making the children's rooms perfect for them but never moved in. It wasn't long afterwards that I left him.

I then started seeing my ex-husband again, dating, which we hadn't done the first time around, but it wasn't really working. We didn't live together again but were together for probably about a year. He hadn't dated anyone during our time apart and clearly loved me, but I couldn't commit myself to him and so walked away and finally began the divorce process. I hurt him all over again. I had relationship after relationship, never choosing someone who was emotionally or physically available. Each relationship was more dysfunctional than the last and it was no accident that this coincided with my increase in drinking, which was now at its height. I spent virtually no time on my own, always having someone waiting in the wings to move on to when the current relationship inevitably failed, although I was not aware of this behavior, it was all driven my need to be validated by someone else. I had no idea how to validate myself and I did not know how sick my behavior was by needing someone else to constantly validate me. I also went through a period where I did have actual one-night stands, sex that didn't progress into a relationship of any kind.

I lost my driving license when I was 33 and was deep in all my then un-diagnosed addictions. I needed validation more than ever due to the immense shame I felt at losing my license. I didn't drink throughout my 18-month ban, but my love addiction continued to gain momentum and went from strength to strength. I was now getting involved with men who were not single. Sometimes I didn't know, because they either didn't tell me or me they lied to me if I questioned them, and some I knew were married or in long term relationships, but I had ceased to care. I needed to get my "fix" which got even worse when I started drinking again after the ban was up. It got to the point where I was drinking to blackout most evenings and incapable of having a relationship. When I did go out and was attracted to someone I was persistent to the point of being a nuisance and humiliated myself on several occasions. I got into recovery for my alcoholism in January 2003, but my love addiction continued to spiral out of control.

It is recommended that we don't get involved with anyone during our first year of recovery in AA, but I ignored that and got involved with someone at 3 months sober. That relationship was also unhealthy because I hadn't made any changes in my behaviors, I was more just a dry drunk at that point. The relationship lasted about 8 months and for the first time in my life I walked away from the relationship without having someone waiting in the wings. I did obsess about various men in AA at this time, but I didn't go after them, which was very new behavior. Looking back, I must have made the men I obsessed about feel very uncomfortable around me. A few months later I got into another relationship with someone who had practically no sobriety at all, which was very wrong of me and is called 13th Stepping in AA. He moved in after about 2 weeks, what on earth was I thinking, and we ended up getting engaged after just a few short months. My gut knew that this was a mistake and when my sponsor questioned me, I started to withdraw from her and ploughed ahead with the relationship even though it was falling apart. My fiancé picked up a drink again and went on a week binge with absolutely no contact and started talking about taking drugs again. I found the strength to walk away even though I was terrified of his temper and potential backlash when I moved his stuff out. I did then spend some time on my own but again was in constant fantasy and obsession.

I was four and a half years sober from booze, 2 years sober from food addiction and a year sober from over exercising when my therapist suggested that I was a sex and love addict. I was absolutely mortified. I didn't want to be a sex addict, but the love addict bit felt more manageable. I didn't understand what she was talking about, until she said sending that first text to the guy to get validation is like picking up that first drink and I then knew exactly what it meant, although I was far from ready to be willing to change my behaviors at this point. It had to get more painful. I had been emotionally enmeshed with men instead of being in an actual relationship with them. I really had no idea how to be on my own. I thought I needed the interest or support of a man to survive life. I eventually went into a treatment centre later that year for my love addiction. I was close to picking up a drink and I was back in my food anorexia because the pain of my behaviors around relationships was intolerable. During my 28-day stay at a primary addiction centre I started working the steps around my sex and love addiction. When I came out of treatment I started going to SLAA meetings and there began my journey into recovery from love addiction. I went to meetings for 10 months and learnt so much about how my disease manifests itself. I was still unwilling to start doing the work necessary to begin my real recovery process in this area of my life. I needed to look at all my past relationships and behaviors and then change my unhealthy behaviors. As a result, I got into a relationship with another recovering addict who I hurt badly as I then moved onto yet someone else before starting the steps. It was recommended that if we are single when we start working the steps, that we stay single until completing Step 9, and I knew from previous step work that it could take me years to get to Step 9 due to much fear-based procrastination. In typical addict fashion I made sure I got into another relationship before I started working the steps, as I still didn't know how to be on my own. It was, I know, very manipulative of me, but I still wasn't ready to go "cold turkey". I did some things right, I attended regular meetings, got a sponsor to help me through the step work and continued to see my counsellor.

I found the step work excruciating at times. Just realizing how many ways my disease manifested itself left me feeling full of shame and guilt, but without this awareness I couldn't set bottom lines - a list of behaviors that were considered "using" that I needed to abstain from. Some were really hard to let go of. Scanning was a big thing for me and I had no idea that I was even doing it before I started going to meetings. After setting "no scanning" as a bottom line I spent about 6 months looking at the ground wherever I went so I couldn't catch someone's eye to see if they were checking me out, to feel validated. I walked into lampposts, letterboxes and people so that I didn't slip on that particular bottom line! The other one I found exceptionally difficult was not allowing obsession and fantasy to fill my mind. I could be walking down the street and see someone who I thought was attractive and build a whole fantasy about this person in my head for days, weeks, even months to avoid the pain of being single. There is a tool called the 3-second rule and at times I would have to work this about every 5 seconds, but if worked it does work. Working the first three steps in my love addiction was intense, painful and very revealing, and took me nearly twice as long as it could have because I slipped (broke my "bottom line" behaviors) twice during this period. Making daily outreach calls was challenging too, it meant that others in recovery would really get to know me and that was very scary, as my fear of being rejected for not being good enough was massive. During the process of working the steps, I came to realise that yet again I had chosen a man who wasn't emotionally available, and it became very painful for me to stay in the relationship. I realized about 9 months into the relationship that I needed to leave but didn't have the courage to do so, until it really got painful enough, which took another 6 months. It felt like the hardest decision I had to make, but I was learning to like myself a little and knew that I needed to walk away even though the thought of being single until I had completed Step 9 felt pretty tough.

The withdrawal from being validated by men was very painful. I felt like I was wading in treacle for months, I was tired all the time and felt very lonely, but I was learning about myself all the time. I started to build relationships with women, and although I previously had female friends, I was very mistrusting of women in general. I saw them as competition. Because I thought I was unacceptable, unlovable, and unworthy, I thought that I wouldn't be noticed if I was around other women. It has been a long slow process, but I now have the most amazing friendships with women I have met through meetings, I feel so privileged and grateful for these women in my life. I slowly plodded my way through the remaining steps and remained single for over 3 years, although I did tentatively try making friends with a man I met through meetings, it didn't work out as we both developed feelings for each other and he then bottom lined me (i.e. he was not allowed to see or contact me). My Step 9 work came and went, and my sponsor started challenging me about dating. I was terrified of dating. I didn't know how to date, and the thought of Internet dating was absolutely terrifying. My life was full with my girlfriends and for the most part I was very happy. Working the SLAA programme helped me to change from being someone who couldn't be on her own, bouncing around from one unhealthy relationship to another to someone who was almost too content being on her own. Both were extremes and I needed to find some balance. My sponsor kept pushing me to date and I was very resistant. Eventually after more time passed I agreed to start internet dating if my Higher Power hadn't put anyone in my path once I got back from my late summer holiday. I was so grateful that my Higher Power saved me from Internet dating when a man I met whilst in treatment contacted me via Facebook. We chatted for a while and in time started dating. This relationship was very different from any other relationship I had ever been in; it bloomed very slowly. Of course, there were issues that needed addressing, but I had tools to help me and a sponsor who supported me and shared her experience with me. I had to learn to ask for my needs and wants to be met, rather than hoping my partner would guess what was going on in my mind. The old me would expect my partner to guess and when he failed to do so I would get angry and resentful that he was not a mind reader. I had to learn to set boundaries. I had to learn to be vulnerable. It was all challenging at times, but worth it in the long run. I was learning about myself and becoming a lot more emotionally healthy. That relationship didn't work out, but I didn't leave it feeling a failure as I had with pretty much every other relationship.

My sponsor had me stay single for a minimum of 6 months so that I could process everything that had taken place in that relationship and take my new healthier behaviors with me into the next. I again spent a while on my own and again was happy doing so. By now I had completed the 12 steps and the maintenance questions but knew that there was still more work to be done. Having put down all my acting out behaviors and bottom lined negative thinking which was a massive part of my SLAA disease and addiction in general, I realized that I needed to work on my anorexia; emotional, social and sexual. Little did I know that this was going to be even more painful than the initial set of SLAA steps I had worked through. I still had so much work to do around believing that I deserved the best that life had to offer, to really get in touch with all my emotions, which, despite being in recovery for over 10 years by this time, were still very scary for me. It was especially challenging for me to learn to really love and nurture myself.

I dated someone briefly about 18 months later and had more insights about relationships and myself. I was then single for a further 4 months, again very happy. A man who had asked me out twice previously, asked again just over 2 years ago and something in me said just say yes, so I did but not knowing why I did. The first time we met for coffee was relaxed and we got on really well, with many similar interests. I left feeling that I wanted to get to know this man better; it was a new and exciting feeling. We started dating and got on very well. I revealed that I was in recovery within a month of dating him; I knew that he was a special man and I needed to know that he would be ok with this before I became too involved. He was very accepting and did some reading up about it for himself. Our relationship went from strength to strength. But eventually, as it had in all my previous relationships, my sexual anorexia reared its ugly head yet again. I was gutted. I really thought that I had done enough work around this, but it seemed not. I started more written work around it, brought it into my therapy sessions and we had a joint therapy session together to help. I was so grateful to my partner for being willing to help me work through what is essentially my problem, but he did also realise that he was bringing his own stuff into the relationship as well. I grew up in a home where crying was not allowed so crying always brought me great shame. I was learning to cry in therapy where it was a safe environment and I was being vulnerable with only one person, who knew me well after 12 years of regular sessions. In our joint session, I did allow myself to cry, well I say allow, my therapist has a way of getting me in touch with feelings which allows the tears to flow, and this session was no different. I had no defense against the tears, despite thinking I would be rejected for crying, instead of being rejected I was comforted by my partner, he had seen me at my most vulnerable and still accepted me; this was such a breakthrough for me, although I still carried much shame. This is ongoing work for me, and us, but we both want our relationship to work so we are doing our best.

Life is tough at the moment, my sister was advised that she has terminal cancer, and because I had allowed my partner to see me cry in therapy, I allowed myself to cry, a lot, when I next saw him, and he continues to be so supportive as do my many friends. I am slowly learning to be vulnerable and authentic and know that I am acceptable and loveable – what a miracle, and it is all down to 12 step programs, my sponsor and fellow recovering addicts, my willingness to keep working on myself and having a relationship with my Higher Power. It's a total roller coaster but I wouldn't change a thing. I am the very best me I can be today, and I am so very grateful.

Alexis Story

I believe my love addiction began at a very early age. I remember being obsessed with a boy all the way through playschool, primary school and secondary school. I used to spend hours in fantasy and projection and found it soothing and comforting during my childhood, as there was little love or emotional support going on at home. I eventually dated this boy when I was 14. When he asked me out it was literally like a lightning bolt that jolted me out of all my pain and misery and rocketed me into another dimension. However, it only lasted a few months, as I was desperately shy and so self-conscious that I could barely speak to him, so he ended it. I went in to what I now know as "withdrawal", I felt completely empty, hopeless, worthless, worse than I had before he ever asked me out. It felt like there was nobody at home to comfort me and I was desperately unhappy. This set the stage for my adult life. I set out to find "the one" in order to chase the "high" that I experienced when my first boyfriend asked me out. I have been through this cycle of "highs" and withdrawal many times since then.

I did have some reasonable relationships in my 20's but I could not commit, as most of them were unavailable men with alcoholic tendencies. The few I dated who were "normal" I found utterly boring so would leave them. The alcoholics who I wanted to stay in a relationship with would leave me. The ones I found 'exciting" never hung around long. I married one alcoholic, but it didn't last too long and by my mid 30's I was pursuing crazier and crazier men just to get the "hit" I needed. I knew there was something really wrong with me but did not know what it was. The final straw for me was when I was stalked for a year by a man I had dated for a short while. I had agreed to marry him after only knowing him for four months and knowing that he had issues with his mental health. This shocked me and woke me up to the fact that I could not go on living like this and sought help in a 12-step group called Sex and Love Addicts Anonymous. I am now 46 and have attended a group since walking into my first meeting. It has been a slow upward climb out of my insanity and addiction. I relapsed after four years when I took my will back and went out with another emotionally unavailable alcoholic. This time it was different and with my sponsors help and the help of the other women in the fellowship I was able to walk away and get back into recovery. I regained my serenity and sense of self and self-worth.

My journey has not been easy. I had to look at my relationship with money (I under earned and was always waiting for "Mr. Right" to come and save me emotionally and financially) and I have done work around my co-dependency. I have also worked on my relationship with "self" with my therapist. I have learned that I cannot look to other people, places or things to soothe me; I had to find how to do that for myself by going within. I had to learn how to love myself first. Today I have a relationship with a higher power, whom I choose to call God. I am not religious in any way, but I do believe that when I hand my "will" over to something greater than me my life gets better, when I take it back and start trying to "run the show" it gets bad petty quickly for me.

I am now in a loving, committed relationship with a man who is emotionally available, and I have not run away. Neither he or the relationship are perfect, but it is most certainly "good enough" and my happiness is not in his hands, my relationship is just one area of my life, rather than the whole of it. I have learned to get my needs met in many different, healthy ways. Everything in my life today, my home, my job, my relationship, long term, honest friendships, I owe to walking through those doors into recovery from my love addiction. I highly recommend it

Chapter 9

Detoxing from an addictive relationship -The Withdrawal Process

At some point, if you have identified that you are indeed a love addict and want to do something about it, then you may want to come out of your current relationship if it is physically, mentally or emotionally damaging to you. Making the decision, whilst hard, is not as difficult as going through the actual withdrawal process. Most people who are love addicts and are not in a programme of recovery of some sort and are facing this issue will not know that the process of withdrawal exists. Most deal with the situation and how they are feeling by going out and getting straight into another relationship, lose themselves in work, food, drink, porn, TV, gambling, anything to distract themselves from the resultant pain of withdrawing from the toxic relationship. It is no easy task and not for the faint hearted, but it is a process that needs to be engaged in if you want to live the life you really want to live, alive, connected to self and others in healthy ways, fulfilled and present in your own life. Here are a few suggestions to help you whilst going through this difficult period. Your love addict mind will tell you that:

- "The relationship was not that bad, I think I will get back in touch".
- "I need someone else to help me get over it".
- "This time it will be different"
- "I feel like I am going insane"
- "I feel depressed, I have no energy to get up and engage with my life"
- "What is the point of living without him/her?"

These are all normal thoughts that you will think at this time. You need to know to expect them and if, and when they occur to let them pass through you and not feel the need to act out on them. If you do "slip" and re-connect with your ex, don't beat yourself up, get back to self-care as soon as possible and try again. The following recommendations may help you to get through this difficult time:

1. Practice Self Care. This means eat healthily. Do not starve yourself or over eat. Try to eat three balanced meals a day, avoid sugar, caffeine (apart from 1 or 2 cups in the morning) and processed food. Many people eat on their feelings or completely starve themselves during this period. Make sure you sleep and relax enough to rest your

body and mind. Try a meditation app such as "Insight timer" or "Omvana" which are free. Daily bathing and ablutions are important, as these are often the first behaviours to disappear when you are distraught and in withdrawal.

2.   Connect with others - resist the temptation to isolate. Make at least one outreach call to someone else that understands what you are going through (not your Ex) every day, at the start of the process, as you need to be talking out not acting out your feelings.

3.   Stay out of fantasy and in reality – don't sit and watch romantic or sexual films or read romantic novels. Although reality is incredibly painful, the emotions will pass, and you will be free of them a lot sooner if you don't get lost in fantasy, but instead feel the feelings and work through them.

    a. .

4.   Do not engage with your qualifier (your EX) unless on a practical matter and it is absolutely necessary, and even then, with no game playing and clear communication.

5.   Make and stick to a structure for each day, no drifting. This is important and will help enormously with the process of withdrawal.

6.   Limit the amount of time you watch TV to an hour or so a day, it is too easy to numb feelings with "electric valium".

7.   Read inspirational literature daily.

8.   Pray (to whatever feels right to you) and meditate daily.

9.   Drink lots of water and herbal tea, limit caffeine intake to the morning and no more than 1-2 cups daily. Avoid alcohol and any other mood-altering drugs, as they will affect your ability to reason.

10.   Take some form of physical exercise daily, resist over exercising to mood alter, everything in moderation right now. A gentle walk outside each day is good.

11.   Connect with others who are in a 12-step programme or those who are spiritually aware for support.

12.   Feed your spirit – for me that means playing guitar and singing, listening to music or going into nature. You identify your own and do it.

13.   Ask for help when you need it. Part of my pattern is not asking for help or allowing others to be there for me. Vulnerability is very difficult. Relying on others is difficult but asking for help is essential.

14.   Bottom line any obsessions, such as voyeurism, promiscuity, flirtation, intrigue and any other behaviour that takes you away from a healthy core.

15.   Deal with paperwork and anything practical you must do.

16.   Be sane with your finances no compulsive over spending or scrimping.

17.   Rest whenever you need to but don't have more than 1 duvet day in a week, as this then becomes avoidant behaviour.

18.   Journal daily, write it out, don't act it out.

19.   Go to a therapist for massage, acupuncture, reflexology, Bowen technique, Reiki or any therapy that works for you. Do not use a sexual masseur.

20.   Have a mantra for yourself that works for you. In times of real pain repeat it over and over again. Things like "this too shall pass", "let go and let God" or "all is well, and all is well".

21.   Do not make any long-term important decisions in this period, as it will be hard to see or think clearly.

22.   Steer clear completely of toxic people or places including bars, strip clubs, fetish clubs or anywhere that can trigger your addiction.

23.   Cut out all mood-altering substances including alcohol, drugs, self - medicated over the

counter drugs or legal highs. You need to go through, not deaden or delay this process. There is only one way through and that is through. If you are on prescribed medication, then follow your G.P.'s advice.

24.   If you can afford it check into a 12-step treatment centre that deals with sex addiction, love addiction and co-dependency.

25.   If you have a talking therapist book extra session whilst going through the process of withdrawal and de-toxification.

26.   Limit or stop social media for a time. Do not under any circumstances join or spend any time on dating sites of any kind, or anywhere you can look for a new potential partner such as Tinder and the like. Block all access to your qualifier. Delete their telephone number and under no circumstances have contact with your qualifier, unless there are children involved and even then, try and do this in the short term through a mediator. If this is not possible email what you need to say and keep it to practical matters only.

You are less likely to get drawn back in through email than on the phone or in person.

27.   Obsession-look out for any signs of obsessive thoughts or actions. If you find yourself in obsession practice the three-second rule – try to think about something else after 3 seconds.

28.   Keep practicing self-care; deal with one thing each day, not everything at once. If you start to feel overwhelmed, stop and breathe, go to a meeting, do an online meeting, outreach for help and above all be gentle with yourself.

29.   Avoid negative self -talk or any abusive behaviour to self

30.   Be patient, give time time.

I will not deceive you here; in withdrawal you can experience some of the most excruciating emotional pain you will ever have to endure. You will want to run and act out, find someone else to distract yourself from the pain, or even worse re-connect with your "qualifier "(your ex). You may want to do the opposite and disappear from the world for days, weeks or even months. You need to keep functioning and connecting with your life as much as possible. There may be days when you literally want to curl up and die. I cannot stress to you how important attending a 12-step group is to get through this. I know 100% for me I would not have made it through this period without one. It is vitally important you connect with and spend time with people who understand what it is you are going through. It is not helpful to be around people who don't get it, who tell you to just "pull yourself together", "plenty more fish in the sea", or who want to talk to you about what your qualifier is up to. There may be times when you think you have lost the plot completely and that you have gone insane. You may have thoughts of suicide or self-harm. You need to talk these out, not act them out. You can and will get through this, but it will not be easy, and you absolutely cannot do it on your own, you need help. If you cannot physically get to a 12-step meeting, there are online meetings.

One day you will move out of the withdrawal process and back into life. You will start to notice colour again, or the birds singing. There will be little glimpses of life returning to your field of vision. You will start to re-inhabit your body and life and will start to take an interest in the world around you again. Bit by bit you will regain your energy and your zest for life. You will be able to start planning and thinking about the future, what possibilities there are for you, travel, return to education, a new job? You may be happy about this, but there may also be deep soul sadness, a weight within you, as you begin to come to terms with how much of your life has been affected and ruled by your love addiction. For some this means they have never been in a loving, long-term, committed relationship, for others they have never had children and may never do so. Some people have no career to speak of as most of their focus has been on the addiction, instead of their career, or they may have the children and the career, but feel a deep sadness and feeling of loss as they realise just how much of their time and head space has been dominated by the need to act out on their addiction. Give yourself time to grieve in this period. Write and talk about these realisations as much as possible. Allow yourself to feel the feelings and if you begin to feel overwhelmed seek out a CBT or similar therapist who can help you get through this very painful but necessary stage in your recovery.

Chapter 10

What is Social, Emotional, and Sexual Anorexia?

One of the most revolutionary ideas I learned in SLAA was the concept of social, emotional and sexual anorexia. Social, emotional and sexual anorectics avoid being with people and relationships, avoid feelings and emotions and avoid sex or physical closeness. For me my anorexia was present in my life in different ways. My emotional anorexia was apparent in terms of my inability to truly allow anyone "in" emotionally. My social anorexia was present throughout my life and showed itself as fear of social situations and groups of people. My ever present sexual anorexia meant that without a mood-altering substance inside of me I found it terrifying to be sexual or have sexual intimacy, and this would always become more apparent the longer I remained in a relationship. The feelings of not being fully present and engaged in my own life, of living behind a wall of ice, and under achieving are also facets of my anorexia. Anorexia shows itself in people in many ways, such as never having a relationship, never getting married or having a family, compulsive busyness, and having lots of acquaintances but no close friendships. For many people it is a constant nagging feeling of being dis-engaged, almost ghost like in one's own life, never being fully present or committed to anything or anyone, including yourself. In terms of sexual anorexia this can mean avoiding sex at all costs, having sex but splitting off and not being emotionally present, being able to have sex at the beginning of a relationship, where there is little real emotional connection and intimacy, to being less and less able to be physically close as the fear of intimacy rises the longer the relationship continues. It is not just about the sex at all it really is about terror of intimacy (in-to-me-see). Most anorectics are terrified that if other people really got to know them, they would run for their lives. They fear being the "hole in the donut", that if someone was to get emotionally close then they will realise that they are not really in a relationship with another person, but with a fake, a shadow, a ghost.

Sexual anorexia within love addiction plays out at the extremes of sexual promiscuity and/or total sexual abstinence. Social anorexia can manifest itself as compulsive business and/or total isolation, and emotional anorexia includes anything from total independence, not allowing anyone in, to total loss of self in another. For the love addict Anorexia equates to a complete disconnect from self. Throughout my whole life I felt like I was an over exposed picture, I lacked an outer sheath of protection, felt things too much and suffered from chronic over sensitivity. A lot of people in recovery form sexual, social and emotional anorexia find this the hardest part of the recovery process. I have seen people cry week after week at meetings as the ice starts to melt and the realisation dawns of how absent they have been from their own lives. The sadness around missed opportunities, for the relationships they never experienced, the family they never had, the career they never pursued and the life left unlived. Recovery is possible from this point. The emotions need to be felt, the pain and the realisation must be gone through to fully heal from this devastating silent killer of dreams. Once recognised and shared in meetings the written work is then an invaluable tool to help you identify exactly what anorexia means to you and how it shows itself specifically in your life. The written work is a declaration that you are at last showing up for your own life. The work will illuminate your patterns and recognising these is a major step forward in beginning a new life where you are connected to yourself firstly and then to others. You will gently challenge yourself to experience new things. There are times when you will want to retreat under the duvet, which is a normal part of the recovery process, but you will no longer live there.

The steps forward will be baby steps at first and each step is a confirmation to yourself that you are a worthy cause, that your life does matter and that you are not the "hole in the donut" but a real person with something to offer to the world.

I would recommend attending SLAA meetings, especially those with an anorectic focus. You may also want to look for a sponsor who has already been through this process and share as honestly and openly as you can to other members of the group. These can become the relationships where you take your first baby steps at letting people in. For me they are still my closest relationships, even though we live in different countries, the bond remains. With your Sponsor you practice letting someone in that you trust. As the trust and honesty grows, you can start allowing others in too. Recovery for anorexia is a slow process, with forward and backward motion, it is not a straight line, but you can do it and it is so worthwhile. You will be able to consciously take risks that would have been impossible before, to start to say "yes" to life. You will be able to practice real self-care where you nourish your body, heart, mind and soul and give it what it really needs. You will no longer have to deny yourself sustenance, rest, friendship, fun and joy. You will be able to set boundaries and value yourself, your time and your space. You will set bottom lines about what your "acting in" or "acting out" behaviours are, and you will no longer engage in them. You will also set top lines around what loving acts you will do for yourself. Above all you will learn to love, respect and be gentle with yourself as you emerge from your cocoon into the sunlight probably for the first time in your life. It can feel scary at times, but with a support system and a higher power (which could be the group) it is possible, and it is so worthwhile. You will not want to miss this part of your recovery and your life.

Chapter 11

What Is Co-dependency and how does it differ from Love Addiction?

The term co-dependency was first used when therapists and counsellors first started working with the families of alcoholics in the USA in the late 20th Century. They were initially referred to as co-alcoholic or co-addict, but this changed, and the term used today is co-dependent. What the therapists who were working with the families discovered was that the disease of addiction affected all the members of the family in many unexpected ways. On a practical level the partners of the alcoholic/addict had often had to assume complete responsibility for the running of the household and finances, as the alcoholic/addict became less and less able to do so. It was on the emotional level that the therapists were most intrigued with what they observed. They found that the co-dependent was almost totally focussed on the alcoholic/addict, at the expense of everything and everyone else, which often resulted in self-neglect. A person who was not co-dependent would have more than likely left the addict/alcoholic long before the destruction and devastation that being with the alcoholic/addict caused to all those around them, but the partners of the alcoholic/addict stayed and stayed. The children of course had no choice, but a high proportion of the children born in these families went on to be alcoholics or addicts themselves or married an alcoholic, an addict, or someone with a gambling, work or sex addiction. It seemed all those whose lives revolved around the alcoholic/addict became addicted to the drama and unpredictability that followed in the alcoholic's wake. A household with addiction is often unpredictable, shame based, and guilt based. It can lead to the members within the family experiencing feelings of inadequacy and confusion, which often resulted in them seeking external validation, as they lacked the internal self-esteem from which to produce their own.

This phenomenon of co-dependency explains why, when the alcoholic/addict became sober, some of the partners left or wanted the alcoholic/addict to drink again. Something much more important was going on other than the need to be in control. It appeared that many of the co-dependents loved to play the role of the martyr, victim or rescuer and when this was no longer possible, found it very difficult to adapt and to take on a healthier role. Alcoholism, addiction and co-dependency were often found to be cross-generational. People pleasing and the inability to say "no", needing to be needed and over commitment with the ensuing resentment are typical co-dependent behaviours. Ultimately these behaviours stem from the co-dependent's inability to love, value and trust themselves. Thus being "other referenced" leads them to trying to fix, control and "help" other people to raise their own low self-esteem. Most of their self-esteem comes from one or more of these traits and whilst not "bad" in themselves, the co-dependent takes them to an extreme that is unhealthy and lose their connection to their own needs. They often have no clue what needs fixing in their own lives and what they need to do to improve their own situation but are more than likely to be able to provide 100 ideas on how you can fix your life. This trait of fixing other people's problems is called "caretaking" and involves doing for others what they could easily do for themselves. Along with low self - esteem the co-dependent is often perfectionistic and self -critical. Whilst they can overlook and make excuse after excuse for the alcoholic/addict in their lives, they are often overly critical of their own faults. Alongside caretaking is the co-dependent trait of being overly responsible for everything, especially other people's happiness. Co-dependents will go way above and beyond what most people would do to make a situation that is ultimately outside of their control, better, usually at their own expense. This is termed "people pleasing" and can lead to the co-dependent overextending themselves and ultimately to burnout. Most co-dependents have trouble setting healthy boundaries. They either build brick walls around themselves or have no boundary at all. The term "needless and want less" is often used to describe the co-dependent. A common script is "if I ... then ..." which could be "if I keep the house perfect then he will love me" or "if I take care of all the bills then he will notice me" ad infinitum.

At the core of co-dependency is often fear and shame. A common trait of co-dependency is passive-aggressive communication. Instead of owning how they feel and being open and honest about this the co-dependent will do almost anything to avoid direct confrontation or to express their own feelings. Often, they communicate in a much more underhand, indirect way such as through subtle insults or behaviour such as sulking. This in turn leaves the other people in communication with the co-dependent feeling the "co-dependent crazies". It is hard work for the people around the co-dependent as the co-dependent constantly fails to speak about their own reality and often projects what they are feeling onto all those around them. To make matters worse, most co-dependents have absolutely no idea that they are doing this, they are in complete denial of how unhealthy their way of being and communication style really is or what effect it has on the people around them. Underneath these traits the co-dependent has a real fear of abandonment. Often abandoned physically or emotionally as a child, the co-dependent has a great need to attach. The problem is that the people they are most drawn to attaching to (the alcoholic/addict) are themselves unable to attach in a healthy way as their primary attachment is to alcohol or their addiction.

I was co-dependent firstly with my mother as I could tell you at 1000 paces what mood she was in, whilst being completely out of touch with my own reality. My childhood was shame based and I felt guilty for my acting out behaviours. There was alcoholism present within my family of origin and secrets around my mother's mental state and behaviour. As I got older the focus of my co-dependency shifted from my mother to my boyfriends. I always abandoned my own wants and needs and put theirs first. I had low self-esteem and little or no self-love. I was bright and capable of achieving so much, felt abandoned and would therefore abandon myself. I fluctuated between having no boundaries at all and massive walls. I oscillated between feeling like I was in control of a relationship then giving up all my needs to be in the relationship. I continue to be aware of any time I revert to passive aggressive communication and choose instead, as much as I can, to communicate honestly, clearly and cleanly with all those I have contact with. I now have healthy boundaries and have criteria for all my relationships, not just my romantic ones.

Although co-dependency and love addiction often go hand in hand, as they did for me, the highs and lows of love addiction are much more pronounced than in co-dependency and the reliance on fantasy is far greater in love addiction. Also, nowhere in the literature on co-dependency does it talk about emotional, sexual and social anorexia, which is at the core of love addiction for many love addicts, which is known as "love avoidance". Love addicts often jump from one relationship to another, overlap relationships or stay in or return to abusive relationships, rather than be on their own. They are constantly in pursuit of "the one" who will fix them and make it all better; they live in fantasy and dream of their "saviour". If they can't find "the one" they will sometimes settle for whoever is there then spend their time doing a makeover on the object of their affection to turn them into "the one", rather than admit that the person is not right for them. Love addicts have "magical thinking" whereby they fantasize about the person they are in a relationship with and turn them into somebody else, then when that person fails to live up to the love addicts unrealistic expectations, they blame them for not doing so. Love addiction is the compulsive pursuit of romantic love as experienced at the infatuation stage of a new relationship. Once the intensity fades, which is a normal part of all long-term relationships; the love addict is then driven to find their next "high". Some will move onto another relationship, others will stay in their original relationship but have multiple affairs.

Another aspect of love addiction is the total disregard the love addict has for any signs and symptoms that the object of their affection is not suitable for them. This was certainly true for me with my children's father; my need to attach was greater than my need to listen to myself and be safe. My initial thoughts about him, that he was moody and aggressive were true, but I totally ignored them at my own cost. I repeated this pattern of behaviour again with my second husband. I knew there were big flaws in his character but ignored my own "red flags". The pursuit of romantic relationships takes the love addict away from their true-life path and much of their time and energy is spent either looking for or keeping a relationship instead of using their energy to pursue their own dreams and goals. It also means they are often left without friends and long-term connections with other people as their focus has been solely on their love relationship. Hence wasted lives, lost opportunities and abandoned friendships. All of this was certainly true for me. When my first marriage ended there was no one left to help me pick up the pieces of my life. My husband had been the sole focus of my attention for nearly 8 years. When the marriage ended I truly was on my own and if I had not done the work on myself that I had done up until that point, I may not have made it. I was self-aware enough to know that I was in deep trouble emotionally and needed outside help. Thankfully I sought out the professional help of a therapist who had themselves done a lot of work on their own love addiction and co-dependency issues and was able to guide me in the right direction.

Love addiction is about your patterns of behaviour around your love relationships. It is not about "him" or "her" but about you and how you operate in all your romantic relationships. It is about the addiction to the high you get from the flush of a new relationship and the resultant feelings of unhappiness and irritability that ensue once that has gone. Ultimately it is about fear of intimacy, which is why "love avoidance" is the flip side of the same coin as love addiction. Both the love addict and the love avoidant fear intimacy. The love avoidant stays out of all romantic relationships, they often choose to remain in fantasy even when presented with an opportunity to act out the fantasy with the object of their affection; the love addict often gets into relationships with emotionally unavailable people such as other addicts or emotionally damaged individuals. If they do manage to get into a relationship with someone who is emotionally present they will often trash that relationship, as they are unable to maintain the illusion of intimacy once the "high" has subsided. Both the love addict and the love avoidant have an inordinate amount of their time, energy and attention spent on "other", both have wasted lives, careers that don't get off the ground and poor relationships with the other people in their lives such as family members or friendships. Both types of people have little or no self-esteem, self-love and self-care; they have abandoned themselves in the pursuit of "other", whether real or imagined. They are not present in their own lives. This explained my experience with my first boyfriend who was a good guy, emotionally present, kind and caring yet I had to walk away. That is not to say that he was perfect by any means, he did after all ask me not to go to University instead of supporting me in my decision to do so, but he was emotionally and physically available and present. As an adult I took the set of beliefs that I was "invisible" unlovable, unimportant and shame based into all my relationships and kept looking for the "other" who could wave a magic wand and fix me. Someone who would love me enough and connect with me enough so that the pain of being me would go away. What happened instead was that the "others" I attracted were themselves broken or damaged, no more able to rescue me than they were to rescue themselves.

Chapter 12

What Is A Healthy Relationship?

Many people come to SLAA (Sex and Love Addicts Anonymous), CoDA (Co-dependents Anonymous), or Al-anon (for those with an alcoholic in their life) in the hope that they get to fix a broken relationship, or find a new, better one. If that is your intention, then you are missing the point completely. The point of recovery is to have a better relationship with you. That is the most important relationship you will ever have in your life and one that we love addicts neglect beyond all measure. Being in recovery means you get to focus on what you want and need for you, how to live comfortably, possibly for the first time in your life, in your own skin. How to love, accept and value yourself as a person, not in a narcissistic way but in a way where you value who you are, your time, your hopes and dreams and you value yourself enough to show up for your own life and commit to whatever it takes to live it fully. Moreover, it is about being your own best friend. Alongside this relationship is the relationship to your higher self; your higher power, God, the Universe, spirit or whatever form this takes for you. If you struggle with this concept it could be your conscience or intuition, the place inside that connects you to good, to truth, to the best version of you. This relationship is essential for your on-going recovery. It is an important part of all 12-step recovery programmes. It has nothing to do with religion, I have known atheists and agnostics who were able to embrace this aspect in their own way, and everything to do with being a better version of you, living with honesty, self-awareness and respect for self and others.

Your other important relationships are with recovery friends and friends who may not be in recovery but are on a spiritual path. You may or may not have on-going relationships with your family of origin, but if you do it will be on a different footing. You may have work relationships and again these may well be on a different footing as you are more present in your life and career. Finally, you may be ready for a romantic relationship. You will have your own criteria about what you are looking for, what is and what is not acceptable, how slow you want to take things. You will date and go out and do non-sexual activities together, just to get to know one another. You will not engage in sex until you are sure you want to commit to a relationship with this person. You will take your time, check in with yourself regularly, carry on with your life regardless and look out and listen for red flags when they occur. You will no longer commit emotionally until you know the person well enough. You will not live together straight away or dive straight in to a sexual relationship. You will hold yourself in regard and esteem yourself. If at any time you feel you are being railroaded, love bombed, rushed, lied to, manipulated or anything else that gives you that uneasy feeling in your stomach you will listen, stop and get out if necessary. You will come from a place of self-awareness, self-love and self-respect so anything that does not feel in alignment with this will be talked about, evaluated and discarded if it does not match up. It is not about perfection but a level of honesty, communication and transparency that you feel comfortable with.

I know if I ever choose to be in a committed loving relationship again, these are the criteria I will use, and nothing less will do. However, for now I have no need to be in a relationship, I am in a relationship with myself, my higher power, my recovery friends, my children, my musical buddies and my friends who are spiritual seekers. My life is full of music, laughter, peace, simplicity, calm and creativity. I have no drama going on as I choose not to engage in any. My hope is that you too find your own place of calm where you are engaged with your life and are not blown off course by other people's ideas about what you "should" or "should not "do. At 47 I went mountain biking in the Alps, at 48 started surfing. I started running at 49 and joined a reggae band at 50. I moved to another country to live at 55 and started playing guitar and singing again after a break of almost 30 years also at 55. I released an album of my own music at 56 and am finishing writing this book having just turned 57. I have also started doing yoga and meditation, which are both important to me and have joined a spiritual development group. Who knows what the future will bring but I do know that it will be great as I am committed and present in my own life, I am confident in my capacity to listen to my own truth and follow it with appropriate action. I know I am more than capable of practicing self-care and having and maintaining long term friendships with both men and women. A man, a job or a label does not define me; I am defined instead by how I live my life today and how I express my love in all aspects of my life. I wish you all a life that is worth living.

Chapter 13

Questions to Diagnose Love Addiction

1. Have you ever tried to control how often you see someone and failed miserably?

2. Do you find yourself unable to stop seeing a specific person even though you know that seeing this person is destructive to you?

3. Do you get "high" from romance? Do you crash afterwards?

4. Have you been in relationships with dangerous people, or put yourself in dangerous situations in the pursuit of "love"?

5. Do you make promises to yourself or rules for yourself concerning your romantic behaviour that you find you cannot follow?

6. Have you been in a relationship with someone you don't (didn't) want to be in a relationship with?

7. Do you believe that a relationship will make your life bearable and that without a significant "other" your life is meaningless?

8. Do you believe that someone else can "fix" you?

9. Do you feel desperation or uneasiness when you are away from your partner?

10. Do you feel desperate about your need for a lover or future mate?

11. Do you have a pattern of repeating bad relationships?

12. Are you in or have you been in a relationship with someone that is clearly physically unavailable i.e. married?

13. Are you in or have you been in a relationship with someone who is emotionally unavailable such as a drug user, workaholic, alcoholic, or someone with a compulsive behaviour such as overeating or over exercising?

14. Do you feel the need to constantly flirt?

15. Do you feel like you are only really "alive" when you are with your partner?

16. Do you use relationships to avoid dealing with life's problems?

17. Are you left feeling exhausted because of your love life?

18. Are you unable to concentrate at work because of your constant thoughts of "other"?

19. Does your life feel unmanageable and out of kilter because of your romantic behaviour and excessive dependency needs?

20. Have you ever felt like you were wasting your life in fantasy when you could achieve so much more?

Chapter 14

Resources:

Recovery Groups: Look online for contact details in your area of the world.

SLAA – Sex and Love Addicts Anonymous
SA – Sex Addicts Anonymous
CoDA – Co-dependents Anonymous
Couples in Recovery Anonymous
RA- Relationships Anonymous
Al-Anon
AA - Alcoholics Anonymous
NA - Narcotics Anonymous
ACoA – Adult Children of Alcoholics
DA – Debtors Anonymous
OA – Overeaters Anonymous

Other Useful Resources that may help you to engage with your life:

Mindfulness
Yoga
Tai Chi
Chi Gung

Meditation Groups
Spiritual Development Groups

Books:

Sex and Love Addicts Anonymous: The Basic Texts for
the Augustine Fellowship
The Vortex – Ester and Jerry Hicks
The Road Less Travelled – M. Scott Peck
Women Who Love Too Much – Robin Norwood
Co-dependant No More – Melody Beattie
Soul Love – Sanaya Roman
Healing the Shame That Binds You – John Bradshaw
Pia Melody – Facing Co-dependence

Made in the USA
Middletown, DE
13 July 2019